T0194769

An Analysis of

Simone de Beauvoir's

The Second Sex

Rachele Dini

Routledge
Taylor & Francis Group

LONDON AND NEW YORK

Published by Macat International Ltd
24:13 Coda Centre, 189 Munster Road, London SW6 6AW.

Distributed exclusively by Routledge
4 Park Square, Milton Park, Abingdon, Oxon OX14 4RN
605 Third Avenue, New York, NY 10017

Routledge is an imprint of the Taylor & Francis Group, an informa business

www.macat.com
info@macat.com

Cataloguing in Publication Data
A catalogue record for this book is available from the British Library.
Library of Congress Cataloguing-in-Publication Data is available upon request.
Cover illustration: Capucine Deslouis

ISBN 978-1-912302-84-0 (hardback)
ISBN 978-1-912127-58-0 (paperback)
ISBN 978-1-912281-72-5 (e-book)

Notice
The information in this book is designed to orientate readers of the work under analysis,
to elucidate and contextualise its key ideas and themes, and to aid in the development
of critical thinking skills. It is not meant to be used, nor should it be used, as a
substitute for original thinking or in place of original writing or research. References and
notes are provided for informational purposes and their presence does not constitute
endorsement of the information or opinions therein. This book is presented solely for
educational purposes. It is sold on the understanding that the publisher is not engaged
to provide any scholarly advice. The publisher has made every effort to ensure that
this book is accurate and up-to-date, but makes no warranties or representations with
regard to the completeness or reliability of the information it contains. The information
and the opinions provided herein are not guaranteed or warranted to produce particular
results and may not be suitable for students of every ability. The publisher shall not be
liable for any loss, damage or disruption arising from any errors or omissions, or from
the use of this book, including, but not limited to, special, incidental, consequential or
other damages caused, or alleged to have been caused, directly or indirectly, by the
information contained within.

CONTENTS

THE MACAT LIBRARY

The Macat Library is a series of unique academic explorations of seminal works in the humanities and social sciences – books and papers that have had a significant and widely recognised impact on their disciplines. It has been created to serve as much more than just a summary of what lies between the covers of a great book. It illuminates and explores the influences on, ideas of, and impact of that book. Our goal is to offer a learning resource that encourages critical thinking and fosters a better, deeper understanding of important ideas.

Each publication is divided into three Sections: Influences, Ideas, and Impact. Each Section has four Modules. These explore every important facet of the work, and the responses to it.

This Section-Module structure makes a Macat Library book easy to use, but it has another important feature. Because each Macat book is written to the same format, it is possible (and encouraged!) to cross-reference multiple Macat books along the same lines of inquiry or research. This allows the reader to open up interesting interdisciplinary pathways.

To further aid your reading, lists of glossary terms and people mentioned are included at the end of this book (these are indicated by an asterisk [*] throughout) – as well as a list of works cited.

Macat has worked with the University of Cambridge to identify the elements of critical thinking and understand the ways in which six different skills combine to enable effective thinking.
Three allow us to fully understand a problem; three more give us the tools to solve it. Together, these six skills make up the **PACIER** model of critical thinking. They are:

ANALYSIS – understanding how an argument is built
EVALUATION – exploring the strengths and weaknesses of an argument
INTERPRETATION – understanding issues of meaning

CREATIVE THINKING – coming up with new ideas and fresh connections
PROBLEM-SOLVING – producing strong solutions
REASONING – creating strong arguments

To find out more, visit **WWW.MACAT.COM.**

CRITICAL THINKING AND *THE SECOND SEX*

Primary critical thinking skill: ANALYSIS
Secondary critical thinking skill: REASONING

Simone de Beauvoir's 1949 book *The Second Sex* is a masterpiece of feminist criticism and philosophy. An incendiary take on the place of women in post-war French society, it helped define major trends in feminist thought for the rest of the 20th century, and its influence is still felt today.

The book's success owes much to de Beauvoir's brilliant writing style and passion, but both are rooted in the clarity of her critical thinking skills. She builds a strong argument against the silent assumptions that continually demoted (and still demote) women to "second place" in a society dominated by men. De Beauvoir also demonstrates the central skills of reasoning at their best: presenting a persuasive case, organising her thoughts, and supporting her conclusions.

Above all though, *The Second Sex* is a masterclass in analysis. Treating the structures of contemporary society and culture as a series of arguments that tend continuously to demote women, de Beauvoir is able to isolate and describe the implicit assumptions that underpin male domination. Her demolition of these assumptions provides the crucial ammunition for her argument that women are in no way the "second" sex, but are in every way the equal of men.

ABOUT THE AUTHOR OF THE ORIGINAL WORK

Born in Paris in 1908, **Simone de Beauvoir** was a gifted scholar whose radical ideas and scandalous love life shocked France and the wider world. She was at the forefront of twentieth-century existentialism—the philosophy that replaced God with personal choice. De Beauvoir was a prolific and high profile writer of philosophy, fiction, and autobiography until her death in 1986. *The Second Sex*, her essential book about what it means to be a woman, inspired the feminist movement.

ABOUT THE AUTHOR OF THE ANALYSIS

Dr Rachele Dini studied at Cambridge, King's College London and University College London. Much of her current work focuses on the representation of production and consumption in modern and contemporary Anglo-American fiction. She has taught at Cambridge and for the Foundation for International Education, and is now Lecturer in English at the University of Roehampton. Her first monograph, *Consumerism, Waste and Re-use in Twentieth-century Fiction: Legacies of the Avant-Garde*, was published by Palgrave Macmillan in 2016.

ABOUT MACAT

GREAT WORKS FOR CRITICAL THINKING

Macat is focused on making the ideas of the world's great thinkers accessible and comprehensible to everybody, everywhere, in ways that promote the development of enhanced critical thinking skills.

It works with leading academics from the world's top universities to produce new analyses that focus on the ideas and the impact of the most influential works ever written across a wide variety of academic disciplines. Each of the works that sit at the heart of its growing library is an enduring example of great thinking. But by setting them in context – and looking at the influences that shaped their authors, as well as the responses they provoked – Macat encourages readers to look at these classics and game-changers with fresh eyes. Readers learn to think, engage and challenge their ideas, rather than simply accepting them.

'Macat offers an amazing first-of-its-kind tool for interdisciplinary learning and research. Its focus on works that transformed their disciplines and its rigorous approach, drawing on the world's leading experts and educational institutions, opens up a world-class education to anyone.'

Andreas Schleicher,
Director for Education and Skills, Organisation for Economic
Co-operation and Development

'Macat is taking on some of the major challenges in university education … They have drawn together a strong team of active academics who are producing teaching materials that are novel in the breadth of their approach.'

Prof Lord Broers,
former Vice-Chancellor of the University of Cambridge

'The Macat vision is exceptionally exciting. It focuses upon new modes of learning which analyse and explain seminal texts which have profoundly influenced world thinking and so social and economic development. It promotes the kind of critical thinking which is essential for any society and economy. This is the learning of the future.'

Rt Hon Charles Clarke, former UK Secretary of State for Education

'The Macat analyses provide immediate access to the critical conversation surrounding the books that have shaped their respective discipline, which will make them an invaluable resource to all of those, students and teachers, working in the field.'

Professor William Tronzo, University of California at San Diego

WAYS IN TO THE TEXT

KEY POINTS

- Simone de Beauvoir was a radical French philosopher and writer.

- *The Second Sex* was an analysis of why women have always had less power and freedom than men.

- De Beauvoir drew on different disciplines to argue that women have been oppressed throughout history, and her book helped to set the feminist* movement in motion.

Who was Simone de Beauvoir?

Simone de Beauvoir was a radical French philosopher, writer, and political activist whose groundbreaking work tackled the underdog status of women and inspired the feminist movement.

Born in 1908, de Beauvoir grew up in a middle-class Parisian family and was a gifted scholar. Her father was a lawyer who encouraged his daughter to study, while her mother was a devout Roman Catholic.* At convent school de Beauvoir considered becoming a nun, but later came to be an atheist and remained one for the rest of her life.

In 1929 she earned a degree in philosophy* at the Paris Sorbonne—also known as Paris University. De Beauvoir was one of only a handful of female graduates. When she was 21 she met the philosopher Jean-Paul Sartre* at the renowned École Normale

Supérieure and they were lovers and friends until his death in 1980. De Beauvoir became a secondary school teacher but was suspended from teaching after a scandal involving accusations that she and Sartre had seduced one of her female students in 1939.

De Beauvoir published her first novel, *She Came to Stay* (based on the scandal), in 1943, and her first philosophical essay, *Pyrrhus and Cinéas*, in 1944. Next came *The Ethics of Ambiguity* (1947) and *The Second Sex* (1949). Her semi-autobiographical novel *The Mandarins* followed in 1954.[1]

In 1972 de Beauvoir declared herself a feminist, revising her previous stance that a socialist* revolution would be enough to emancipate* women.[2] She died of pneumonia in 1986 and is buried beside Sartre in the cemetery of Montparnasse in Paris.

What Does *The Second Sex* Say?

De Beauvoir's book tackles women's social status from the beginning of civilization to the modern day. Her central argument is that women have been forced to take a secondary role to men since the earliest times, and that the whole human condition is viewed in male terms and is described in language that excludes women.

De Beauvoir makes her case using three frames of reference. The first is historical materialism,* which addresses the influence of social and economic conditions and class on shaping history. De Beauvoir also employs existentialism*—the philosophy that emphasizes personal freedom and choice in a world where there is no God or other higher power. Then she brings psychoanalysis* to bear in examining the underlying (known as "subconscious") causes of human behavior.

De Beauvoir's historical materialist investigation shows how women have been trapped into dependence on men in every area of their lives, ensuring they have no real power in culture or society. She highlights how society treated women as legal minors, very like children. This frustrated their ability to take part in public life on an equal footing with men. For these reasons, women are largely absent from the great stories of history. Men have always been granted greater economic, political, and social power, so they have also had more influence on cultural and historical events.[3]

Viewing the female lot through an existentialist lens, de Beauvoir argues that femininity is constructed. By this she means that a person's nature depends on outside forces. This is the complete opposite of the traditional philosophical view that human nature is fixed at birth. As an existentialist, de Beauvoir argues that human beings are not born with any particular values and create an identity only as a result of their circumstances. *The Second Sex* famously states that no one is born a woman, but rather becomes one through how she is raised and treated by society.

Throughout history, de Beauvoir argues, women have been cast as the "Other."* This is a philosopher's term for that which is separate or distinct from the human self. De Beauvoir argues that society views women as the "Other," because they are viewed only in relation to men. They are treated as objects of desire for men, as mothers to their future heirs, or as the ones who look after everyone else. Denying women their own subjectivity (the right to view themselves as individuals) with their own perspective is dehumanizing* and leaves them powerless.

Psychoanalysis is used in *The Second Sex* to expose the contradictions and untruths in myths* about femininity that are to be found throughout art, literature, religion, and popular culture. De Beauvoir argues that cultural understandings of femininity have no basis in fact. Instead they are rooted in male fear and male desire. They express men's longing to possess, own, and achieve in the world. Women's sole purpose in society is to satisfy such male longings. The female role in these myths is passive. Without men pursuing them, seducing them, or making them their wives, women have no reason to exist.

Why Does *The Second Sex* Matter?

The Second Sex is a milestone in the study of women's experience in society and is regarded by some as marking the birth of feminism. De Beauvoir's resounding achievement was to show the full extent of the sexism* at work in modern society. Her broad vision and use of critical tools from several disciplines were put to work methodically in making her case across all areas of literature, culture, and scholarship.

De Beauvoir tackled head on the accepted, centuries-old beliefs about women's place in the home and the function of marriage. She questioned the very idea of femininity. The book stirred up a storm of controversy in the conservative France of 1949, and de Beauvoir was criticized and ridiculed both for her ideas and her private life. However, *The Second Sex* set decades of debate in motion about patriarchical* (male-centered) attitudes that endures to this day.

It is also true that to a twenty-first century reader, many of de Beauvoir's theories may seem to be stating the obvious. Radical books like *The Second Sex* are often doomed to having their ideas seem dated to future generations. By calling the status quo into question, the book helped to bring about change. That some parts of the text have become obsolete could be regarded as achieving the desired result. This means aspects of de Beauvoir's analysis will feel out of date and some of her demands (such as her call for all women to work) may have been overtaken by questions about how it is possible to both work and raise children.

At the same time, de Beauvoir's work as a whole remains intensely relevant to modern debate. *The Second Sex* is still consulted for its contribution to core areas of academic and social concern. These include de Beauvoir's emphasis on how male power is built on cultural myths. And the messages society feeds girls about femininity is still a matter for concern more than half a century after she first identified the problem.

The work is still a highly original approach to how we define gender and sexual orientation. It also stands alone for its historical importance. This is the text that paved the way for the feminist movement and helped to launch the fight for women's rights* in France, the United States, and around the world.

NOTES

1 Simone de Beauvoir, *She Came to Stay*, trans. Roger Senhouse and Yvonne Moyse (New York: W. W. Norton & Co., 1954); *Pyrrhus et Cinéas* (Paris: Gallimard, 1944); *The Ethics of Ambiguity*, trans. Bernard Frechtman (New York: Citadel Press, 1996); *The Mandarins*, trans. Leonard M. Friedman (New York: W. W. Norton & Co., 1991).

2 Elizabeth Fallaize, *Simone de Beauvoir: A Critical Reader* (London: Routledge, 1998), 6.

3 Simone de Beauvoir, *The Second Sex*, trans. H. M. Parshley (New York: Alfred A. Knopf, 1953), 123.

SECTION 1
INFLUENCES

MODULE 1
THE AUTHOR AND THE HISTORICAL CONTEXT

KEY POINTS

- *The Second Sex* was written just after World War II* and was a groundbreaking account of women's oppression from the beginning of human history to the present day.

- Both de Beauvoir's intellectual environment and her lover, the philosopher Jean-Paul Sartre,* played a role in shaping the work.

- She was influenced by the anti-colonialist* and American Civil Rights* movements, by postwar discussions about anti-Semitism,* and by the recent gains of French women in the workforce.

Why Read this Text?

The Second Sex by Simone de Beauvoir was first published in 1949 and is regarded as a landmark feminist* manifesto. Its unprecedented analysis of female status throughout history triggered decades of discussion around how sexism* governs the lives of women.

De Beauvoir uses a series of theoretical approaches to tackle the origins and wide-reaching effects of female oppression and the work has been a key text in the women's rights movement.* It is partly thanks to *The Second Sex* that we now acknowledge women's contribution to the workforce and accept that some women do not want children.

De Beauvoir was the first thinker to suggest that a person was not born with a gender identity but acquired one through the influence of society and culture. This idea is fundamental to the disciplines of queer

> ❝ What is a woman? … The fact that I ask it is in itself significant. A man would never get the notion of writing a book on the peculiar situation of the human male. But if I wish to define myself, I must first of all say: "I am a woman"; on this truth must be based all further discussion. ❞
>
> Simone de Beauvoir, *The Second Sex*

theory* and gender studies.* De Beauvoir's assertion that "One is not born, but rather becomes a woman" is among the most famous statements in feminist theory. [1]

The Second Sex takes an interdisciplinary* approach to exploring the force of cultural myths* and how ideas about femininity affect child development. The book is an enduring work of scholarship that is still important in the modern debate around the status of women.

Author's Life

Simone de Beauvoir was born in Paris in 1908 and grew up in a wealthy middle-class family. She was raised a Roman Catholic,* but became an atheist at the age of 14. She excelled in her studies and took a degree in philosophy,* becoming one of only nine women to graduate from the famous Sorbonne University in Paris in 1929.

After university, de Beauvoir sat in on courses at the prestigious college for academics and civil servants called the École Normale Supérieure, even though women had not yet been admitted to the institution. It was here, aged 21, that she met fellow philosopher Jean-Paul Sartre. De Beauvoir went on to teach at a secondary school in the French city of Rouen, and she and Sartre became a couple. De Beauvoir was opposed to marriage and they never had children. They also had an open relationship, which was a controversial arrangement for the time. Scandal erupted when allegations were filed against de

Beauvoir for sexual misconduct against a female student. The student's parents accused de Beauvoir and Sartre of acting together to seduce their 17-year-old daughter in 1939.

The allegations—raised much later—led to de Beauvoir being suspended from teaching in 1943. Her first novel, translated in English as *She Came to Stay* (1943), was a fictionalized account of a similar affair. She published her first philosophical essay, *Pyrrhus and Cinéas*, in 1944, and *The Ethics of Ambiguity* in 1947. *The Second Sex* in 1949 was followed by the novel *The Mandarins* in 1954, which won France's most prestigious literary prize, the Prix Goncourt.

De Beauvoir spent her later years writing travel essays and a four-volume autobiography. In 1972 she declared herself a feminist for the first time, revising her earlier claim that a socialist* revolution would be enough to liberate women.[2] She campaigned for women's rights both in France and the United States until her death in 1986.

Author's Background

De Beauvoir's work was shaped by the aftermath of World War II and the radical beliefs that fueled a number of different ideas, including Marxism,* existentialism,* and the Civil Rights movement.*

Marxism is a political theory based on the works of the nineteenth-century philosopher and social theorist Karl Marx.* Marx said that by pursuing profit, the economic system of capitalism* created class inequality and encouraged the exploitation of labor. De Beauvoir was influenced by the Marxism of the Soviet Union,* where leader Joseph Stalin* ran a centrally planned economy. Stalin claimed his system eliminated social classes and private property by making all resources public under state control.

Many on the French Left, including de Beauvoir, believed that a socialist revolution* was key to solving postwar France's economic woes. She modeled her idea of female freedom on her perception of women's role in the newly formed Soviet Union. However, de

Beauvoir was unaware of the Soviet Union's cruel treatment of its workers, many of whom were held in labor camps. Stalin's system was later criticized for being completely at odds with the principles of Marxist thought.[3]

Existentialism was a philosophical movement made famous by Sartre, de Beauvoir's partner, in the 1940s. It emphasized the existence of the individual, along with freedom of choice. In *Existentialism is a Humanism* (1946), Sartre reversed the traditional idea that a person is born with an identity. He argued instead that "existence precedes essence" and that "man first of all exists, encounters himself, surges up in the world—and defines himself afterwards."[4] He meant that human identity is not fixed and is a product of circumstance. De Beauvoir argued that if identity is socially constructed then femininity is also created the same way.

De Beauvoir believed that existentialism could be used to liberate women. France had only granted women the right to vote in 1944 as more women joined the workforce when men went to fight in World War II. One of her concerns in *The Second Sex* was to cement and build on the powers women had gained during the war.

De Beauvoir's work was also influenced by the French anti-colonialist movement[5] that was fighting to end the oppression of France's minority groups. The Malagasy Uprising* in 1947 raised public awareness of oppression in French colonies. In *The Second Sex* de Beauvoir contrasts the solidarity felt between ethnic minorities fighting their oppressors to the attitude of women, which is actually complicit with their oppressors. She looks at the way women feel more solidarity with their fathers and husbands than they do with other women. For this to change, de Beauvoir says they must switch their loyalty and join together with other women. According to her, without solidarity the fight for women's freedom will fail.

NOTES

1   Simone de Beauvoir, *The Second Sex*, trans. H. M. Parshley (New York: Alfred A. Knopf, 1953), 249.

2   Elizabeth Fallaize, *Simone de Beauvoir: A Critical Reader* (London: Routledge, 1998), 6.

3   Alfred B. Evans, *Soviet Marxism-Leninism: The Decline of an Ideology* (Westport, CT: Praeger, 1993), 163.

4   Jean-Paul Sartre, "Existentialism and Humanism," in *Jean-Paul Sartre: Basic Writings*, ed. Stephen Priest (New York: Routledge, 2002), 28.

5   Margaret A. Simons, *De Beauvoir and* The Second Sex*: Feminism, Race, and the Origins of Existentialism* (New York: Rowman & Littlefield, 1999).

MODULE 2
ACADEMIC CONTEXT

KEY POINTS

- *The Second Sex* is not confined to a single academic field and in it de Beauvoir draws on history, philosophy* and literature.

- The work tackles human freedom and the role of social structures in creating either freedom or oppression.

- De Beauvoir built her arguments about the role of women by using elements of existential humanism,* Marxist* historical materialism,* and Lacanian psychoanalysis.*

The Work In Its Context

In *The Second Sex*, Simone de Beauvoir takes a broad interdisciplinary approach to her work that draws on philosophy, history, and literary criticism.* This is necessary because a woman's life adds up to more than her sexuality, her biology, or her economic status. In the book she says, "The categories of 'clitorid' [clitoris] and 'vaginal', like the categories of 'bourgeois'* or 'proletarian',* are equally inadequate to encompass a concrete woman."[1]

De Beauvoir's project was highly original. Before *The Second Sex* appeared in 1949 the examination of women in history, culture, and society was glaringly absent. Scholars who addressed the condition of women were largely ignored and were only reclaimed from obscurity by feminist* scholars in the 1970s. These neglected thinkers included the philosopher Mary Wollstonecraft,* the socialist writer August Bebel,* and anthropologists* Johann Jakob Bachoffen* and Lewis Henry Morgan.*

Wollstonecraft's 1792 work *A Vindication of the Rights of Woman*

> ❝ The whole of feminine history has been man-made. Just as in America there is no Negro problem, but rather a white problem; just as anti-Semitism* is not a Jewish* problem, it is our problem; so the woman problem has always been man's problem. ❞
>
> Simone de Beauvoir, *The Second Sex*

argued that, like men, women should receive an education. Later contributions from Bebel, Bachoffen, and Morgan that specifically addressed the broader social role of women were only recognized when feminist scholarship emerged from the mid-1970s onward.[2] Little attention was paid to Morgan and Bachoffen's claims that prehistoric and early modern societies were based on matrilineal* lines, meaning that people were identified in relation to their mothers.[3]

Before the 1960s few humanities scholars outside of history departments explored the position of women, with the notable exception of English novelist Virginia Woolf.* In her essay *A Room of One's Own* (1929) Woolf argues that Shakespeare's* success was a product not only of his talent but of the freedom he was granted as a man.[4] But like Bebel and the German philosopher and political theorist Friedrich Engels* before her, Woolf's views did little to shift public opinion about women.

Overview of the Field

De Beauvoir's historical analysis of women's oppression draws heavily on Marxist historical materialism. This approach to history was developed by the political theorists Karl Marx* and Friedrich Engels and focuses on the role of class struggle, social inequality, and the exploitation of labor. Engels saw the role of women in society through a historical materialist lens. De Beauvoir was inspired by Engels's argument that throughout history women were objects of exchange, or commodities, and that capitalist* ideologies reinforced this. Engels viewed marriage as a series of financial transactions between the bride's father and the groom. Similarly, de Beauvoir's central idea is based on Bebel's argument in *Women and Socialism* that woman "is the first human being which came into servitude. Women were slaves before men."[5]

Engels and Bebel saw women's emancipation*—their gaining of freedom from oppression—as something that would enable a socialist revolution,* but de Beauvoir reversed the equation. For her, a socialist revolution would enable women's emancipation: "A world where men and women would be equal is easy to visualize, for that precisely is what the Soviet* Revolution promised."[6] In other words, where Engels and Marx make women a tool for revolution, de Beauvoir makes revolution a tool for women. But she also argues that historical materialism's ability to explain women's experience is limited by its materialist focus, which "reduc[es] men and women to no more than economic units."[7]

De Beauvoir also developed her ideas in direct opposition to a branch of psychoanalysis*—a system of theory and therapy devoted to understanding the mind—developed by the Frenchman Jacques Lacan.* She took issue with Lacan's concept of the mirror stage. This says children learn to view themselves as fully formed individuals when they recognize their reflection in a mirror. De Beauvoir argued that this is not true for female children as little girls are taught from an early age to look and act in the way others want them to. When a girl looks in the mirror she doesn't see herself; she sees a projection of the expectations of the outside world. These include aspiring to "look like a picture" by "compar[ing] herself to princesses and fairies."[8]

De Beauvoir also challenges the psychoanalytic theory of penis envy.* This holds that female development from childhood to womanhood is marked by a recognition in adolescence that they are lacking a penis. De Beauvoir identified this theory as another male view and argued "these theories themselves should be submitted to psychoanalysis."[9]

Academic Influences

De Beauvoir explains female oppression by using existentialist philosophy to fill the gaps left by historical materialist and psychoanalytic theory. An existentialist approach, she argues, takes into account the "total situation" of women. A woman is "a human being in quest of values in a world of values."[10] In other words, a woman is more than a body or an economic unit.

The central argument of *The Second Sex* is that women are viewed as objects through which men understand the world. De Beauvoir frames this argument in existentialist terms. Existentialism holds that human beings have the capacity to forge their own destinies, and can define themselves on their own terms. De Beauvoir extends this idea to argue that women have the capacity to overcome their secondary status, and define themselves independently from men. In her autobiography de Beauvoir credits Sartre as the inspiration for this approach, but scholars disagree over the extent of his role.[11]

The book also draws on the work of eighteenth-century German philosopher Georg Wilhelm Friedrich Hegel.* He described the human condition as a negotiation between "subject" (the person) and "Other"* (that which is different or alien to the person). De Beauvoir argues that society views humanity purely in male terms and so relegates women to the role of "Other." Women are defined socially and sexually in relation to men and in the way that they are different (or "Other") to men: "Woman … finds herself living in a world where men compel her to assume the status of the Other."[12]

De Beauvoir used Hegelian dialectic*—that is, putting seemingly contradictory ideas together to reach a higher truth—to show that female identity is constructed negatively. As human beings we regard ourselves as essential because we experience the world in relation to ourselves. But society teaches women that they are *in*essential. She says: "The whole drama of woman lies in this conflict between the aspirations of every subject (ego)—who always regards the self as essential—and the compulsions of a situation in which she is the inessential."[13] Women are perceived as inferior simply because they are not men and that is why society treats a woman as a negative version of a man.

NOTES

1   Simone de Beauvoir, *The Second Sex*, trans. H. M. Parshley (New York: Alfred A. Knopf, 1953), 91.

2   Joan Kelly-Gadol, "The Social Relation of the Sexes: Methodological Implications of Women's History," in *Feminism and Methodology: Social Science Issues,* ed. Sandra G. Harding (Bloomington and Indianapolis: Indiana University Press, 1987), 22.

3   Kelly-Gadol, "The Social Relation of the Sexes," 23.

4   Virginia Woolf, *A Room of One's Own* (London and New York: Penguin, 2002).

5   August Bebel, *Women and Socialism*, trans. Meta L. Stern (New York: Socialist Literature Company and Co-operative Press, 1910 [1879]).

6   De Beauvoir, *The Second Sex*, 652.

7   De Beauvoir, *The Second Sex*, 54.

8   De Beauvoir, *The Second Sex*, 264.

9   De Beauvoir, *The Second Sex*, 221.

10   De Beauvoir, *The Second Sex*, 84.

11   Edward Fullbrook and Kate Fullbrook, *Sex and Philosophy: Re-thinking de Beauvoir and Sartre* (London: Bloomsbury, 2008).

12   De Beauvoir, *The Second Sex*, xxviii.

13   De Beauvoir, *The Second Sex*, xxviii.

THE PROBLEM

KEY POINTS

- *The Second Sex* was a call to action to scholars and the public to rethink their assumptions about women and their role in society.

- It challenged established ideas in psychoanalysis,* philosophy,* and history to ask a completely new question: what are the causes and effects of female oppression?

- De Beauvoir's open interest in female sexuality was unusual at the time and her own unconventional sex life led to some personal criticism.

Core Question

Simone de Beauvoir did not write *The Second Sex* in response to an existing debate. She wrote it to open up a brand new area of inquiry and asked big questions: What is a woman? When we talk about humanity, why do we say *man*kind?

De Beauvoir wanted to discuss society's very definitions of gender. That meant examining the far-reaching implications of women's secondary status at home, at work, in politics, and in culture generally. Her views on female sexuality and reproduction marked a radical departure from those of contemporary psychologists* and sociologists,* while her ideas on female subjectivity (the freedom to be an individual) were entirely new to philosophy.

De Beauvoir believed that women should play a full part in academic inquiry. She was convinced that allowing the study of the human sciences to be conducted only by the male half of the species leads at best to a skewed understanding of humanity and at worst to

> 66 One is not born, but rather becomes, a woman. No biological, psychological, or economic fate determines the figure that the human female presents in society; it is civilization as a whole that produces this creature, intermediate between male and eunuch, which is described as feminine. Only the intervention of someone else can establish an individual as an *Other.* 99
>
> Simone de Beauvoir, *The Second Sex*

major misrepresentation.

In *The Second Sex* De Beauvoir systematically challenges and disproves commonly held notions about women on a social, psychological, and biological level. She even goes so far as to question scientists' assumptions about female anatomy, including the reproductive system and sexual desire. In doing so she opened the door to an entirely new set of questions among scholars and in wider society: "How can a human being in a woman's situation attain fulfillment? What roads are open to her and which are blocked? How can independence be recovered in a state of dependency?"[1]

The Participants

The Second Sex challenges established ideas in the fields of psychoanalysis, philosophy, and history. First, de Beauvoir argues that the challenges women face are not internal, as claimed by psychoanalysis. Women's challenges are external and the biggest obstacles to self-fulfillment are to be found in culture and social context. "The very language of psychoanalysis suggests that the drama of the individual unfolds within him … But a life is a relation to the world, and the individual defines himself by making choices through the world about him. We must therefore turn toward the world to find answers."[2]

Second, de Beauvoir does not believe that a woman's destiny is mapped out from childhood. Psychoanalysis lays great emphasis on early events and traumatic memories from which we supposedly cannot escape. Historical materialism,* meanwhile, suggests our path in life is dictated by economic circumstances. De Beauvoir acknowledges the influence of both these factors but argues that women have the power to overcome them. This idea builds on the existentialist* concept of free will. "In order to explain her limitations it is woman's situation that must be invoked and not a mysterious essence; thus the future remains largely open."[3]

Third, de Beauvoir challenges the habit of psychoanalysts to relate women's psychological maturity to their anatomy. For example, she challenges psychoanalysts' view that clitoral orgasms (rather than vaginal) are a sign of sexual immaturity.[4] She links the opinion to the fact that a clitoral orgasm can be had without a man and has no reproductive function. Vaginal orgasm "consigns woman to man and childbearing … put[ting] woman into a state of dependency upon the male and the species."[5] For de Beauvoir, psychoanalysis's diagnosis of clitoral orgasm as "juvenile" is simply an effort to control female sexuality.[6]

The Contemporary Debate

Few of de Beauvoir's contemporaries were interested in female oppression and *The Second Sex* drew on the work of an earlier generation of writers and thinkers. These included Marxist* historians August Bebel* and Friedrich Engels,* who saw the emancipation* of women as key to the success of socialism.* De Beauvoir's work relates these earlier, neglected ideas about women's oppression under capitalism* to the political concerns of her own era.

The only thinker from de Beauvoir's own generation to share her vision was her partner Jean-Paul Sartre.* Like de Beauvoir, Sartre's interest in women's oppression was rooted in a Marxist and existentialist view of social alienation* where class, wealth, race, and religion all play a role in marginalizing certain people. His writings on oppression included *Anti-semite and Jew* (1946) about persecution of Jewish* people, and *Orphée Noire* (1948) about the anti-colonialist* poetry of black intellectuals in the French *négritude* * movement.[7]

De Beauvoir was politically involved in the anti-colonialist movement and was a committed socialist* until the revelations about Soviet* forced labor camps in the 1950s. After World War II,* de Beauvoir was particularly interested in human rights and social equality, as were many on the French political Left. Yet *The Second Sex* was a sharp criticism of the Left's failure to take the emancipation of women as seriously as that of the French colonies and the Jewish people.

De Beauvoir's interest in the nature of female sexuality was shared by American sexologist* Alfred Kinsey.* But Kinsey was openly critical of *The Second Sex*, arguing it had little to contribute to the public's understanding of sexuality.[8] Kinsey shared a similar public image to de Beauvoir. He too attracted both deep curiosity and outrage from a conservative society that was not used to talking so openly about sex.

Kinsey's books *Sexual Behavior in the Human Male* (1948) and *Sexual Behavior in the Human Female* (1953) received a lot of attention in the United States.[9] Both de Beauvoir and Kinsey were openly criticized for their unorthodox sex lives (Kinsey's involved sleeping with his subjects),[10] and controversy over their private affairs was used to discredit their work. Kinsey having sex with his subjects was seen as an abuse of power. De Beauvoir's acknowledged role in persuading some of her young students to sleep with Sartre was first criticized as improper, and later as a form of subservience that contradicted her feminist* views.[11]

NOTES

1   Simone de Beauvoir, *The Second Sex*, trans. H. M. Parshley (New York: Alfred A. Knopf, 1953), xxix.

2   De Beauvoir, *The Second Sex*, 44.

3   De Beauvoir, *The Second Sex*, 672.

4   De Beauvoir, *The Second Sex*, 71.

5   De Beauvoir, *The Second Sex*, 71, 426.

6   De Beauvoir, *The Second Sex*, 71, 426.

7   Jean-Paul Sartre, *Anti-semite and Jew: An Exploration of the Etiology of Hate*, trans. George Becker (New York: Schocken, 1948); "Orphée Noire," in *Anthologie de la nouvelle poésie nègre et malgache de langue française*, ed. Leopold S. Senghor (Paris: Presse Universitaires de France, 1977).

8   Wardell Pomeroy, *Dr Kinsey and the Institute for Sex Research* (New Haven, CT: Yale University Press, 1982), 279.

9   Alfred C. Kinsey et al., *Sexual Behavior in the Human Male* (Bloomington: Indiana University Press, 1975); *Sexual Behavior in the Human Female* (Bloomington: Indiana University Press, 1998).

10   James H. Jones, *Alfred C. Kinsey: A Public/Private Life* (New York: Norton, 1997).

11   Jo-Ann Pilardy, "Feminists Read *The Second Sex*," in *Feminist Interpretations of Simone de Beauvoir,* ed. Margaret A. Simons (University Park: Pennsylvania State University Press, 1995), 40, n. 7.

MODULE 4
THE AUTHOR'S CONTRIBUTION

KEY POINTS

- Simone de Beauvoir's *The Second Sex* addresses women's oppression through the ages.

- Her critique of marriage, analysis of the social and economic factors stacked against women, and revelations about the myths* of femininity helped to fuel the feminist* movement.

- *The Second Sex* highlights how cultural myths about women are deeply rooted in all areas of culture.

Author's Aims

Simone de Beauvoir wrote *The Second Sex* to reveal the full extent of women's oppression and to show how sexist* myths about femininity pervade every corner of society. To do this she divided the book into two parts. Book One was titled *Facts and Myths*, and Book Two was *Women's Life Today*.

Book One examines the history of female subjugation,* or how women have been brought under control. De Beauvoir begins with how different academic disciplines (including biology and psychology*) helped maintain gender stereotypes. The second section shows how women throughout history have been denied "concrete" freedoms, by which she means actual rights such as owning property or taking part in politics. De Beauvoir argues that without concrete freedoms women cannot see themselves as individuals. The belief that women were "inessential" prevented them from claiming the right to concrete freedoms. The end of Book One throws a spotlight on myths

> **❝** The historical and literary culture to which [the little girl] belongs, the songs and legends with which she is lulled to sleep, are one long exaltation of man. It was men who built up Greece, the Roman Empire, France, and all other nations … Children's books, mythology, stories, tales, all reflect the myths born of the pride and the desires of men; thus it is that through the eyes of men the little girl discovers the world and reads therein her destiny. **❞**
>
> Simone de Beauvoir, *The Second Sex*

about femininity in the work of five authors: Henry de Motherlant,* D. H. Lawrence,* Paul Claudel,* André Breton,* and Stendhal.* All share the same message: "that woman freely recognizes [Man] as her destiny."[1]

In Book Two, de Beauvoir moves on to the enduring legacy of the ideas discussed in Book One. Each section examines a stage of womanhood (childhood, adolescence, marriage, motherhood) or a cultural female figure (the prostitute, the lesbian, the single woman). De Beauvoir works through these stages and roles, challenging established ideas about each one. So in the chapter on homosexuality, for example, de Beauvoir criticizes the diagnosis of lesbianism as a form of arrested development that manifests itself in women who have not attained full sexual maturity. Some psychologists of the time suggested that lesbianism was merely evidence that a woman had not matured beyond adolescence.[2] De Beauvoir argues instead that lesbianism is, in fact, a rejection of society's expectation that women should marry and have children: "Woman's homosexuality is one attempt among others to reconcile her autonomy* with the passivity of her flesh." Put simply, it is a refusal to be penetrated and conquered by a man and to bear his children.[3]

Approach

De Beauvoir explains that throughout history women have been objects of exchange between fathers and husbands. The father gives his daughter to her husband with a dowry* of money or land, to compensate for the cost of supporting her. The husband takes the bride because she will have his children. Working women earn less than men because it is assumed their income is simply additional to what her husband earns. For these reasons "men have always held the lot of woman in their hands; and they have determined what it should be, not according to her interest, but rather with regard to their own projects, their fears, and their needs."[4]

De Beauvoir also shows how girls are brought up to want to be wives and mothers. Playing with dolls teaches girls to identify with the doll: "the little girl pampers her doll and dresses her as she dreams of being dressed and pampered; inversely, she thinks of herself as a marvelous doll."[5] She learns that "to please she has to be 'pretty as a picture'; she tries to resemble an image."[6] In this way, the little girl develops "the need … to be admired and to exist for others."[7]

For de Beauvoir, only existentialist* thought can really shed light on these ideas, for it allows women to conceive of themselves in terms other than those that have been imposed on them from their social context. The basic existentialist idea of free will—which says human beings can shape the course of their own lives—provides a way for women to liberate themselves from the constraints and pressures of society at large: "Underlying all individual drama … there is an existentialist foundation that alone enables us to understand in its unity that particular form of human being which we call a human life."[8]

Women's oppression is rooted in society's view of women not as individuals but as "an existent who is called upon to make herself object."[9] All this can change, though. Since femininity is learned it can also be unlearned. Sexual inequality is not founded on how bodies are different, but on how those differences are explained. Women who challenge the interpretation can take control of their lives. De Beauvoir's existentialist approach offers a way to understand the roots of women's oppression and also a way to overcome it.

Contribution In Context

One of the most original and enduring achievements of *The Second Sex* is the way it challenges long-held cultural myths about women and proves that they are embedded in all areas of culture, from literature and art to psychology. De Beauvoir warns that academics are not immune to these myths because they are also part of wider culture.

She highlights popular myths such as the evil stepmother (who seduces a widower and enslaves his children) and the highly sexed woman (who refuses to settle down with one man) that turn up time and again in Western culture, including in medical assessments and psychiatric profiles. She points out that there is no term for the male equivalent of *nymphomania*, used by doctors to describe excessive sexual desire in women. Such terms reinforce the notion that such sexual desire in a woman is abnormal.

Among de Beauvoir's most original and important insights is that the various expectations of women are incompatible with each other. A woman cannot be sexy seducer, virgin saint, self-sacrificing mother, child-like *ingénue*,* and timid housewife all at the same time. Trying to achieve this impossible task means women cannot cultivate independent or coherent identities of their own.[10].

NOTES

1   Simone de Beauvoir, *The Second Sex*, trans. H. M. Parshley (New York: Alfred A. Knopf, 1953), 172.

2   De Beauvoir, *The Second Sex*, 381.

3   De Beauvoir, *The Second Sex*, 382.

4   De Beauvoir, *The Second Sex*, 119.

5   De Beauvoir, *The Second Sex*, 304.

6   De Beauvoir, *The Second Sex*, 304.

7   De Beauvoir, *The Second Sex*, 304.

8   De Beauvoir, *The Second Sex*, 54.

9   De Beauvoir, *The Second Sex*, 381.

10 De Beauvoir, *The Second Sex*, 185.

SECTION 2
IDEAS

MAIN IDEAS

KEY POINTS

- Simone de Beauvoir's *The Second Sex* argues that the world has always been run for the benefit of men.

- De Beauvoir insists that women must be treated as equal to men if civilization is to advance.

- She traces the long history of women's secondary status, argues they are effectively treated as objects, and examines what lies behind popular ideas about what it is to be female.

Key Themes

In *The Second Sex*, Simone de Beauvoir looks at the broad sweep of history to chart the oppression of women from earliest times to the modern day. She argues that the world is run for the benefit of men first and women second.

Her challenge to this patriarchal* society has several themes—sexual equality, female objectification* (treating women as objects), socio-economic unfairness, and how cultural myths* influence the way people behave and think.

De Beauvoir sets out to analyze gender relations* in every area of life. She covers the home and the workplace, the social sphere and politics, literature and art, religion and popular culture. She writes about the roots of women's status as secondary citizens, then explores what their oppression means for society as a whole.

The book investigates deep-seated beliefs about femininity, showing how women are taught from childhood to view themselves negatively in relation to men. Her analysis of gender relations shows

> **❝** To recognize in woman a human being is not to impoverish man's experience ... To discard the myths is not to destroy all dramatic relation between the sexes ... it is not to do away with poetry, love, adventure, happiness, dreaming. It is simply to ask that behavior, sentiment, passion be founded upon the truth. **❞**
>
> Simone de Beauvoir, *The Second Sex*

how women's lives are shaped by the ambitions and desires of their fathers, brothers, and husbands: "To pose woman is to pose the absolute Other,* without reciprocity, denying against all experience that she is a subject, a fellow human being."[1] Traditional institutions such as marriage, de Beauvoir argues, result in women's enslavement by relegating them to the roles of wife, mother, servant, and caretaker.

De Beauvoir's main argument is that these oppressive forces are not only damaging to women, but to society as a whole. She proposes that equality between the sexes is *necessary* for human progress, and that female emancipation* would benefit all society. In *The Second Sex* she champions egalitarianism,* the belief that all humans should be treated the same way. She insists that women and men are not inherently different, but that society treats them as being different.

Exploring The Ideas

The Second Sex argues that women have been oppressed since the beginning of the human race. This makes the fight for emancipation (or liberation) twice as difficult because, unlike Jewish* people or African Americans, women have no previous experience of freedom and no shared history.[2]

De Beauvoir shows that women have never held domestic and public influence at the same time. For example, she notes how in Ancient Greece women had legal powers such as the right to buy or sell property but they had virtually no power in the home. The women's quarters were at the back of the house, and mothers had no control over their children's upbringing.[3] Women in Ancient Rome, by contrast, had no legal powers but inhabited the central quarters of the home, and had limited powers such as the right to manage the servants and their children's tutors. For de Beauvoir, these instances show that women's legal freedom comes at the expense of domestic freedom, and domestic freedom comes at the expense of legal freedom. Only men have both.

This means "woman's place in society is that which man assigns to her; at no time has she ever imposed her own law." And since men have greater economic, political, and social power, they also play a more prominent role in cultural and historical events. De Beauvoir observes, "it is not the inferiority of women that has caused their historical insignificance: it is rather their historical insignificance that has doomed them to inferiority."[4]

De Beauvoir argues that this inferior status influences all aspects of a woman's experience. Building on the existentialist* idea that identity is produced rather than being something that is inside of us from the very start, de Beauvoir argues that "one is not born, but rather becomes a woman."[5] In other words, femininity is learned. The criteria for defining femininity also ensure that women see themselves as inferior.

For de Beauvoir, femininity is a social construct* with a political subtext. That means our understanding of feminine behavior is influenced by custom, culture, and language, all designed to underline women's inferior status to men. We associate femininity with physical weakness and emotional vulnerability, reinforcing the belief that women are unsuitable for the workforce or for positions of leadership.

Language And Expression

De Beauvoir saw herself first and foremost as a writer of novels and autobiographies. It may be the reason why her philosophical* writings are much more accessible than those of her contemporaries. Compared with the work of fellow thinker and de Beauvoir's partner Jean-Paul Sartre,* her writing is largely free of jargon. She assumes little knowledge of psychoanalysis* or existentialist thought on the reader's part, and explains tricky theoretical concepts clearly before giving her reasons for opposing them.

For English-language readers, the text's main challenge is how it was abridged. The original French version of *The Second Sex* is more than 900 pages long, but the book's first translator, H. M. Parshley,* cut out nearly 300 pages. He left out significant chunks of two of its most important sections, including the one on history and the essay on marriage.

Philosopher Margaret Simons* argued that Parshley, a zoologist, was not qualified to translate a book on philosophy and the book suffered as a result. For one thing, Parshley frequently used language that undermined de Beauvoir's arguments. For example, he translated the French word for "humanity", *humanité*, as "mankind."[7] He also mistranslated a number of important philosophical concepts. The existentialist term de Beauvoir and Sartre used to define human consciousness, *etre-pour-soi*—whose standard English translation is "being-for-itself"—implies the potential for free will. Parshley translated it as various versions of "in accordance with one's true nature," distorting its meaning.

Although these issues did not necessarily reduce the work's impact on mainstream audiences (existentialism would, after all, have been quite foreign to them), it did affect the work's critical reception and how it was used by English-speaking philosophers.[8]

For decades, de Beauvoir's English-language publishers Alfred A. Knopf shrugged off requests by French scholars for a new translation, complete with the missing sections. It was only in 2009 that a new English-language version appeared. In 2012 an updated edition of *The Second Sex* was published with previously absent material—including the many biographies of women from history that Parshley left out. However, these new editions were also heavily criticized by de Beauvoir scholar Toril Moi* for allegedly mistranslating the original text.[9] It is important than any reader studying the text in translation is at least aware of these issues.

NOTES

1   Simone de Beauvoir, *The Second Sex*, trans. H. M. Parshley (New York: Alfred A. Knopf, 1953), 238.

2   De Beauvoir, *The Second Sex,* xviii.

3   De Beauvoir, *The Second Sex*, 124.

4   De Beauvoir, *The Second Sex*, 71.

5   De Beauvoir, *The Second Sex*, 122.

6   De Beauvoir, *The Second Sex*, 249.

7   Margaret A. Simons, "The Silencing of Simone de Beauvoir: Guess What's Missing from *The Second Sex*," *Women's Studies International Forum* 6, no. 6 (1983): 559–664. See also Margaret A. Simons, "*The Second Sex*: From Marxism to Radical Feminism," in *Feminist Interpretations of Simone de Beauvoir,* ed. Margaret A. Simons (University Park: Pennsylvania State University Press, 1995), 243–62.

8   Simons, "*The Second Sex*."

9   Toril Moi, "The Adulteress Wife," *London Review of Books* 32, no. 11 (February 2010), accessed February 2, 2015, www.lrb.co.uk/v32/n03/toril-moi/the-adulteress-wife.

MODULE 6
SECONDARY IDEAS

KEY POINTS

- *The Second Sex* is also an examination of the images of womanhood that appear in all areas of culture, especially those that push the idea that motherhood and sexuality are mutually exclusive.

- De Beauvoir suggests that women who do not conform to society's norms are generally viewed as "wild" and need to be tamed.

- She equates the taking of a woman's virginity with a man's need to assert his power. This line of thought can be traced to issues regarding female genital mutilation* today.

Other Ideas

The Second Sex by Simone de Beauvoir takes a close look at related cultural myths* that underpin our understanding of female sexuality. First among these is the myth of the mother and the whore. De Beauvoir puts the power of this myth down to society's reverence for motherhood—and the attitude that motherhood and sexuality are mutually exclusive.

Throughout history and across cultures, women's main purpose has been seen to be to marry and bear their husbands' children.[1] The mother is revered because she helps the species to continue by having children, while women who reject motherhood are stigmatized or characterized in a negative sense. Promiscuity and infidelity by women undermine the institutions of marriage and motherhood,[2] so these women are labeled whores.[3] "The unwed mother causes scandal and for the child the birth is a stain,"[4] while unfaithful wives have been

> **❝** One of the most basic problems of woman ... is the reconciliation of her reproductive role and her productive labor. The fundamental fact that from the beginning of history doomed woman to domestic work and prevented her taking part in the shaping of the world was her enslavement to the generative function. **❞**
>
> Simone de Beauvoir, *The Second Sex*

burned alive or stoned to death.

De Beauvoir points out that society does not hold men to these same standards. "Man, for reasons of prudence, vows his wife to chastity, but he is not himself satisfied with the regime imposed upon her."[5] This is because society recognizes that "marriage kills love" and that husbands are prone to regard their wives "less as a sweetheart than as the mother of their children."[6] Infidelity and prostitution are merely seen as useful means of sexual release for frustrated husbands. The saying that "prostitutes are to the city what sewers are to a palace"[7] conveys the practical function of prostitution. Like the sewers that cleanse a palace, ensuring inhabitants don't end up festering in their own filth, prostitutes allow married men to regularly "expel" their sexual frustrations to keep their marriage intact and society functioning. "The prostitute is a scapegoat; man vents his turpitude upon her."[8]

For de Beauvoir, the mother, the whore, and the prostitute operate in relation to one another to preserve the institution of marriage. "It is in contrast to the sanctified woman that the bad woman stands out in full relief."[9] The myth of the whore is based in the idealization of motherhood. In the same way the "caste of 'shameless women'"—prostitutes—"allows the 'honest woman' to be treated with the most chivalrous respect."[10]

Exploring The Ideas

De Beauvoir also reveals how all of the qualities associated with female emancipation*—strength of character, independent thought, resistance to authority—have been combined in the figure of the wild woman that society wants to domesticate.[11] But society also appreciates that conquest is more enjoyable when the opponent or prey puts up a fight. So the opinionated woman is allowed to voice her ideas not because society wants to hear them, but because it wants to enjoy silencing her. "Man is master of a reality all the more worthy of being mastered in that it is constantly evading control."[12]

De Beauvoir shows how this myth creeps into literature, where a man is often pitted against a spirited female who ends up submitting to his will. She cites William Shakespeare's* *The Taming of the Shrew* (1590–3)* where the male protagonist Petruchio uses psychological* ploys to win over and tame the strong-minded Katerina. In the end, Katerina is tamed into submission and Petruchio "calls his neighbors in to see how authoritatively he can subdue his wife."[13]

Historical figures of female emancipation such as the suffragette* (who fought for the right to vote) and the bluestocking* (a term for female intellectuals) have been similarly viewed as wild animals to be domesticated. De Beauvoir notes that a woman seeking emancipation has to be perceived either as a shrew—a particularly assertive woman— or as a source of sexual attraction. Either way, she risks not being heard for what she is really demanding—liberation.

Overlooked

While de Beauvoir's take on motherhood and sexual desire have been examined extensively, her reading of the myth of virginity has largely been overlooked. This area warrants further study, given its relevance to current discussions about female genital mutilation (FGM). This ritual is practiced in a number of African, Asian, and Middle Eastern countries, as well as among populations in other parts of the world. It is done to control women's sexuality. Clitoridectomy (the amputation of the external part of the clitoris) is designed to prevent female pleasure, while infibulation (the sewing up of the labia) is supposed to preserve a woman's virginity until marriage. This marks her as a closed space to be opened up by her husband. The symbolic meanings attached to FGM cast a new light on *The Second Sex* and its treatment of the virgin.

De Beauvoir equates the act of taking a woman's virginity with power. The virgin is an object of desire the man wishes to have all to himself: "The surest way of asserting that something is mine is to prevent others from using it."[14] Also, as "nothing seems to a man to be more desirable than what has never belonged to any human being," de Beauvoir makes an explicit connection between taking a woman's virginity and the annexing of unoccupied land.[15] These are ways a man "proves" himself through the act of possession.

Taking a woman's virginity allows man to reaffirm himself. "Man fulfills himself as a being by carnally possessing a being."[16] In primitive times, marriage was a form of abduction: "in taking his wife by force [the husband] demonstrates that he is capable of annexing the wealth of strangers and bursting the bounds of destiny."[17] For de Beauvoir, the act of sex is associated with violence and with power. In the same way, FGM is based on the myth of the virgin, enforcing the idea that women are objects of exchange or conquest and that their bodies need to be governed.

NOTES

1 Simone de Beauvoir, *The Second Sex*, trans. H. M. Parshley (New York: Alfred A. Knopf, 1953), 523.

2 De Beauvoir, *The Second Sex*, 178.

3 De Beauvoir, *The Second Sex*, 177.

4 De Beauvoir, *The Second Sex*, 177.

5 De Beauvoir, *The Second Sex*, 523.

6 De Beauvoir, *The Second Sex*, 524.

7 De Beauvoir, *The Second Sex*, 95.

8 De Beauvoir, *The Second Sex*, 524.

9 De Beauvoir, *The Second Sex*, 179.

10 De Beauvoir, *The Second Sex*, 524.

11 De Beauvoir, *The Second Sex*, 143.

12 De Beauvoir, *The Second Sex*, 164.

13 De Beauvoir, *The Second Sex*, 95.

14 De Beauvoir, *The Second Sex*, 143.

15 De Beauvoir, *The Second Sex*, 143.

16 De Beauvoir, *The Second Sex*, 131.

17 De Beauvoir, *The Second Sex*, 68.

ACHIEVEMENT

KEY POINTS

- With *The Second Sex*, Simone de Beauvoir succeeded in drawing attention to the inferior social status of women and why they were largely missing from academia, literature, art, and politics.
- The book was truly groundbreaking for its radical views, leading to the Roman Catholic Church* placing it on a list of forbidden books.
- The book can be seen as dated, but this only shows how successfully de Beauvoir's ideas changed society.

Assessing The Argument

Simone de Beauvoir's *The Second Sex* is an unprecedented attack on how society forces women into a subordinate position. The text sheds light on how sexism* is woven throughout human history and it draws attention to the absence of women in academic fields such as philosophy,* psychology,* and history.

Many of de Beauvoir's arguments were entirely new and challenged the conservative values of postwar France. When discussing the low number of female university graduates, de Beauvoir highlights a survey in which the majority of female respondents agreed that "boys are better than girls: they are better workers."[1] De Beauvoir argues that women are brought up to view themselves as less capable than men and this limits their ambitions and chances of success. A working woman considers it "meritorious enough if she earns her own living [for] she could have entrusted her lot to a man."[2]

The book began a radical new discussion around what women

> **❝** It is not [women's] inferiority that has caused
> their historical insignificance: it is their historical
> insignificance that has doomed them to inferiority. **❞**
> Simone de Beauvoir, *The Second Sex*

could hope to achieve outside of the home. While it would be another 20 years before French women gained either prominence in the workplace, the book's publication was an important step towards the liberation of women from traditional roles.

De Beauvoir was also the first writer to openly challenge society's assumptions about women's sexuality. "It is claimed that woman needs sexual activity less than men: nothing is less certain," she tells us in her chapter on social life.[3] These beliefs, she argues, stem from the fact that "the love act is still considered a *service* woman renders to man, which therefore makes him seem her master."[4] Elsewhere she says that abortion and contraception are a right. Women are entitled to sexual pleasure and should have the freedom to choose if and when to have children.[5] These claims challenged France's deeply ingrained ideas about marriage and sexual relations and

Achievement In Context

De Beauvoir's work was a significant achievement not only for the rigor of its argument and the strength of its ideas, but for its sheer audacity. The book's explicit content and radical views were completely at odds with the intense conservativism and pronatalism* (the championing of having children) of the period.

The Vichy regime* that governed France during World War II* from 1940 to 1944 only reluctantly allowed women to work, and made the distribution of contraceptives a punishable offence.[6] Housewife Marie-Jeanne Latour was executed by guillotine in 1943 for performing abortions.[7] Although women's role in the French

Resistance* against the Nazi* occupation gained them the right to the vote, both the Roman Catholic Church and the government continued to stress the importance of motherhood and family. For a woman such as de Beauvoir to discuss female sexuality and to openly question how desirable it was to have children was shocking.

The way de Beauvoir examined gender relations* and her explicit account of the female orgasm—depending not on biology, but on "the whole situation lived by the subject"[8]—were seen as an affront to sexual morality. The fact that she saw the radical sexologist* Alfred Kinsey's* assessment of female masturbation as limited, arguing that it was, in fact, "much more widespread"[9] than even he claimed, shows just how extreme her views were for the time.

The book's explicit content led the Vatican to place it on the Index of Forbidden Books,* where it remains to this day.[10] De Beauvoir also received angry letters from male readers who called her everything from "unsatisfied" and "frigid" to "nymphomaniac" and "lesbian."[11] At the same time, the book clearly had an effect on mainstream society. Interviews conducted decades after publication reveal how many French women read it in secret and were informed by its ideas.[12] In English-speaking countries the response to *The Second Sex* was less hostile. This was partly due to the less prominent role of the Roman Catholic Church, and partly because British and American readers did not view it as a personal attack on their culture, as French readers had.[13]

Limitations

The Second Sex is a product of its time and was published before important events such as the invention of oral contraception, the legalization of abortion in France, the sexual revolution, and the gay rights movement.* It was written when women were a minority of the French workforce and were seldom seen graduating from university. The role of women in society has changed radically since that time and few readers today will find the book as shocking as its first audiences did in 1949.

Yet the fact that de Beauvoir's book has dated can be seen as a clear indication of its success. *The Second Sex* effectively wrote itself into history precisely because it challenged and then changed Western society. Thanks to de Beauvoir's efforts, Western women live in a world that is very different from the one she describes.

The Second Sex has drawn criticism from some French feminists who see it as hostile to women. De Beauvoir was a devotee of egalitarianism,* intent on dismantling socially constructed* differences between people. For her, femininity is a construct and men and women are not different. Biology is not destiny. Second-wave feminists* in France from the 1960s, such as Luce Irigaray,* Hélène Cixous,* Antoinette Fouque,* and Julia Kristeva,* saw de Beauvoir's efforts to ignore gender difference as forcing women to assimilate patriarchal* values and become men.

As this generation of French feminists reclaimed traditional female activities as valid forms of experience, it distanced itself from de Beauvoir. Today de Beauvoir's work is applied less in her home country than in the United States and Britain.[14] After her death in 1986, Fouque suggested that now de Beauvoir was buried, French feminism could forget her "universalist, egalitarian, assimilatory and normalizing feminist positions" and move into the twenty-first century.[15]

NOTES

1   Simone de Beauvoir, *The Second Sex*, trans. H. M. Parshley (New York: Alfred A. Knopf, 1953), 658.

2   De Beauvoir, *The Second Sex*, 658.

3   De Beauvoir, *The Second Sex*, 521.

4   De Beauvoir, *The Second Sex*, 521.

5   De Beauvoir, *The Second Sex*, 464.

6   Toril Moi, *Simone de Beauvoir: The Making of an Intellectual Woman* (New York: Oxford University Press, 1994), 187. See also Francine Muel-Dreyfus, *Vichy et L'Éternel Feminin* (Paris: Editions du Seuil, 1996).

7   Sheila Rowbotham, "Foreword," in Simone de Beauvoir, *The Second Sex*, trans. Candace Borde and Sheila Malovany-Chevalier (New York: Vintage, 2009).

8   De Beauvoir, *The Second Sex*, 71.

9   De Beauvoir, *The Second Sex*, 71.

10   Elizabeth Ladenson, "Censorship," in *The Book: A Global History*, ed. Michael F. Suarez and H. R. Wooudhuysen (Oxford: Oxford University Press: 2013), 173.

11   Sonia Kruks, *Simone de Beauvoir and the Politics of Ambiguity* (Oxford: Oxford University Press, 2012), 48.

12   Catherine Rodgers, "The Influence of *The Second Sex* on the French Feminist Scene," in *Simone de Beauvoir's* The Second Sex*: New Interdisciplinary Essays*, ed. Ruth Evans (Manchester: Manchester University Press, 1998), 67.

13   Margaret A. Simons, "The Silencing of Simone de Beauvoir," *Women's Studies International Forum* 6, no. 6 (1983): 559–664.

14   Moi, *Simone de Beauvoir*, 97–8.

15   Moi, *Simone de Beauvoir*, 97.

MODULE 8
PLACE IN THE AUTHOR'S WORK

KEY POINTS

- With the benefit of hindsight, de Beauvoir believed that the views she held in *The Second Sex*, though very radical in 1949, had in fact not been militant enough.

- De Beauvoir suggested her partner Jean-Paul Sartre* first pushed her to examine women's social conditions. Scholars have since questioned this view.

- Despite her many works of fiction and memoir, *The Second Sex* remains de Beauvoir's most famous and well-regarded work.

Positioning

Simone de Beauvoir began work on *The Second Sex* in 1946, three years after the publication of her first novel, *She Came to Stay*. She wrote the book in 14 months while working on another essay titled *The Ethics of Ambiguity*, and published extracts of *The Second Sex* in *Les Temps Modernes*,* the journal she founded with her partner and fellow thinker Jean-Paul Sartre in 1945.

The Second Sex marked a relatively early point in de Beauvoir's career, coming before much of her feminist activism. De Beauvoir did not even declare herself a feminist* until much later, in 1972, when she joined the *Mouvement de libération des femmes* (Women's Liberation Movement).*[1] In an interview with feminist publisher Alice Schwarzer that same year, titled "The Revolutionary Woman," de Beauvoir said that *The Second Sex* had not been militant enough. De Beauvoir had believed socialism* could emancipate* women and there was no need for a feminist struggle. She changed her mind when

> **❝** I am merely presenting the reality of what happens to women in our society. It is up to my readers to profit from their mistakes, to learn from their experiences and to keep themselves free from situations that end in the same way. **❞**
>
> Simone de Beauvoir, cited in Deirdre Bair, *Simone de Beauvoir: A Biography*

she saw that socialism had done as little for women as capitalism* had.[2]

In another interview with John Gerassi in 1976, de Beauvoir also said *The Second Sex* was too theoretical and was limited by its focus on the conditions of white, middle-class women and her own personal experiences. What she believed feminism now needed was a book "rooted in practice" and authored by "a whole group of women, from all sorts of countries, and amassed from all classes."[3]

De Beauvoir also revised her view that solidarity among women was difficult to achieve in the face of women's loyalty to their husbands. She did so after witnessing strikes by female factory workers in the 1960s. When their husbands complained, working-class women came together to rebel: "they became committed to a double struggle: the class struggle against the [factory] bosses, the police, the government, etc., on the one hand, and the sex struggle against their own husbands."[4]

Integration

In her 1963 autobiography *Force of Circumstance*, de Beauvoir actually recalls a moment of revelation when she understood that "this was a masculine world" and her childhood had been "sustained by myths* invented by men."[5] She suggests it was her partner and fellow existentialist* writer Jean-Paul Sartre who urged her to examine the social condition of women.

Scholars such as Margaret Simons* and Edward and Kate

Fullbrook* have recently questioned the truth of this account. De Beauvoir's diaries, published after her death, suggest she had been applying existentialist thought to the condition of women as early as her postgraduate days studying philosophy* at the École Normale Supérieure in Paris.[6] *The Second Sex* can therefore be seen as either the beginning of de Beauvoir's feminism, or her first attempt to articulate her ideas in public.

Either way, the book stands out for its important contribution to existentialist thought and the way it mixes philosophical analysis with autobiographical reflection, always a defining feature de Beauvoir's work. De Beauvoir never claimed to be unbiased. She used her experiences as a woman to fuel the work with her own anger.[7]

Like *She Came to Stay* (1943), and later *The Mandarins* (1954), *The Second Sex* was addressed to an audience that knew about her unorthodox views on sexuality and her open relationship with Sartre. Her cultivation of this radical image affected the response to *The Second Sex* in both positive and negative ways. It led to intense controversy but also cast her as a heroine and a symbol of sexual freedom.[8] For her supporters, de Beauvoir's open, childless relationship with Sartre proved that women could aspire to something beyond marriage or motherhood.

Significance

The Second Sex is de Beauvoir's best-known work. While her novels and early essays are restricted to the fields of literary criticism* and philosophy, *The Second Sex* has influenced scholarship in fields as diverse as sociology,* history, and political science.* It also informs branches of study such as feminist historical studies and queer theory.*

Within political science, Gill Underwood and Khursheed Wadia have written about de Beauvoir's views on French feminism's difficult relationship with institutional politics, and her efforts, as a member of the *Mouvement de libération des femmes,** to legalize abortion without resorting to party politics.[9] For these academics *The Second Sex* offers an important jumping-off point for considering French feminism's history of anti-parliamentarism—that is, the rejection of and effort to overturn political institutions.

The Second Sex also remains an important document for Anglo-American feminist critics, who apply its ideas in the discussion of women's rights,* both in lecture theaters and the wider world. Influential American feminists such as Camille Paglia* and Judith Butler* credit de Beauvoir with having an important influence on their work.[10] De Beauvoir's ideas are to be found in many introductions to feminist thought, especially those on being "made" a woman and the role of reproduction in oppression.

Feminist scholar Frederika Scarth uses de Beauvoir's analysis of women's reproductive role as socially produced to consider how "the enslavement of the species that women experience on a biological level, and in the situation of early nomadic societies, is reproduced illegitimately within patriarchy."*[11] What this means is that women's biological role as mothers is used to restrict them within specific arenas such as the home, and to deny other aspects of their identity. Scarth uses de Beauvoir's ideas to discuss the politics of motherhood. More recently, in *Women in Philosophy: What Needs to Change?* (2013), Karina Hutchison and Fiona Jenkins* identify *The Second Sex* as the first attempt to ask why women were left out of philosophical debate. They argue that the situation has not changed: "the exclusion of women, or, put differently, the fostering of men" in the discipline remains a pressing concern.[12] De Beauvoir's work remains relevant to these contemporary debates.

NOTES

1   Claire Laubier, *The Condition of Women in France: 1945 to the Present—
    A Documentary Anthology* (London: Routledge, 1992), 19.

2   Alice Schwarzer, *After the Second Sex: Conversations with Simone de
    Beauvoir* (London: Pantheon, 1984).

3   John Gerassi, "Interview with Simone de Beauvoir: *The Second Sex*, 25
    Years Later," *Society* (January–February 1976), accessed May 5, 2015,
    www.marxists.org/reference/subject/ethics/de-beauvoir/1976/interview.htm.

4   Gerassi, 'Interview with Simone de Beauvoir."

5   Jean Leighton, *Simone de Beauvoir and Women* (Madison, NJ: Farleigh
    Dickinson University Press, 1975), 24.

6   Nancy Bauer, 'Must We Read de Beauvoir?" in *The Legacy of Simone de
    Beauvoir*, ed. Emily Grosholz (New York: Oxford University Press, 2004), 125.

7   De Beauvoir, "Interview."

8   *Daughters of de Beauvoir.* Film produced by Penny Foster, 1988.

9   Gill Underwood and Khursheed Wadia, *Women and Politics in France: 1958–
    2000* (London and New York: Routledge, 2000), 156.

10 Camille Paglia, *Sex, Art, and American Culture: Essays* (New York: Penguin
    Books); Judith Butler, *Gender Trouble: Feminism and the Subversion of
    Identity* (London: Routledge, 1990).

11 Fredrika Scarth, *The Other Within: Ethics, Politics and the Body in Simone de
    Beauvoir* (New York: Rowman & Littlefield, 2004), 141–2.

12 Karina Hutchison and Fiona Jenkins, *Women in Philosophy: What Needs to
    Change?* (Oxford: Oxford University Press, 2013), 9.

SECTION 3
IMPACT

THE FIRST RESPONSES

KEY POINTS

- When *The Second Sex* appeared in 1949 many critics attacked the book as an outrageous insult to the sexual morals of the day.

- De Beauvoir was openly ridiculed and insulted in France, but English-speaking readers were more receptive to her ideas.

- There has been a lot of fierce debate about exactly how much influence *The Second Sex* had on the French feminists* who came after de Beauvoir.

Criticism

French society after World War II* was deeply conservative. Simone de Beauvoir's direct challenge to social and sexual propriety in *The Second Sex* sparked such fury that Roman Catholic* novelist François Mauriac* used it as the basis for a campaign against decadence in literature.[1] An article in a conservative newspaper called the book a "disgusting apology for sexual inversion and abortion."[2]

The French political Left dismissed the book as a work of bourgeois* (middle-class) decadence. It was criticized for "exalting the lowest in man: bestial instincts, sexual depravity"[3] and left-wing philosopher Albert Camus* said it made French men look ridiculous.[4] However, according to de Beauvoir's friend, the anthropologist* Claude Levi-Strauss,* this was because "A *woman* existentialist* was more than [the establishment] could bear."[5]

This generally negative view of the text has endured in France, as critics have argued that de Beauvoir's own role, in soliciting and

> ❝ In actuality the relation of the two sexes is not quite like that of two electrical poles, for man represents both the positive and the neutral, as is indicated by the common use of *man* to designate human beings in general, whereas woman represents only the negative, defined by limiting criteria, without reciprocity. ❞
>
> Simone de Beauvoir, *The Second Sex*

seducing younger women for Jean-Paul Sartre, undermined her feminist principles.[6] She stands accused of failing to recognize the disrespectful treatment of both herself and other women by her lover, the philosopher Sartre, since in seducing these women and passing them on to Sartre, she made herself a tool for Sartre's pleasure, and an accessory to their exploitation. She also stands accused of exploiting younger women, since the student she seduced in 1939 was underage, and of trying to abolish laws on the age of sexual consent.[7] Jean-Raymond Audet described *The Second Sex* as a work of profound "narcissism."*[8] Intellectual interest in *The Second Sex* in France today is rare, with the notable exception of feminist philosopher Michèle Le Doeuff.* In *Hipparchia's Choice* (1990) she examines *The Second Sex* in the context of de Beauvoir's difficult relationship with philosophy* and in relation to Sartre's well-documented contempt for women.[9]

The Second Sex had a warmer reception in Britain and America. Of the 20 books on de Beauvoir published between 1980 and 1992, 17 were in English.[10] The first English-language study of her work, Elaine Marks's* *Simone de Beauvoir: Encounters with Death* in 1973, also introduced *The Second Sex* to a wider readership.

These scholars suggest that French criticism of de Beauvoir often reads as a thinly veiled dislike of women. The Norwegian American feminist writer Toril Moi* notes, "The implication is that whatever a woman says, or writes, or thinks is less important than what she *is*."[11]

So painting de Beauvoir as a narcissist or as Sartre's slave effectively depoliticizes her, reducing *The Second Sex* to the rants of an overemotional woman.[12]

Responses

Soon after *The Second Sex* appeared, de Beauvoir stopped going out to avoid being harassed in the street by angry readers.[13] She was not too surprised. Her publisher rejected an earlier collection of short stories because of its explicit sexual content. She also lived through the outcry against her first novel, 1943's *She Came to Stay*, a fictionalized account of her and Sartre's affair with two of de Beauvoir's female students.[14]

Yet this uproar made *The Second Sex* famous, winning de Beauvoir attention from publishers in the United States and public-speaking roles at home and abroad over many years. The most noteworthy was a 1975 televised interview, "Why I am a Feminist," where she returned to her central theme: "Being a woman is not a natural fact. It's the result of a certain history. There is no biological or psychological* destiny that defines a woman as such … Baby girls are manufactured to become women."[15]

The Second Sex was first published in 1949, and in December of that year de Beauvoir found herself in the throes of an ideological crisis following a United Nations* revelation that the Soviet Union* had been detaining thousands of citizens in forced-labor camps. The news shattered de Beauvoir's faith in socialism* as the way to end class inequality.[16] She broke with the French Communist Party and tackled her crisis in 1954's *The Mandarins*. In 1972 she publically abandoned the belief that a socialist revolution* would bring sexual equality and declared herself a feminist. This revised outlook informed the activism of her later years. She said any follow-up to *The Second Sex* needed multiple authors and a practical approach. Feminism "must derive [its] theory from practice, not the other way around" and must reflect the needs of all classes and cultures.[17] De Beauvoir never gave up on egalitarianism,* though, and was suspicious of differential feminism, the idea that men and women are equal but also different. For de Beauvoir "it falls again into the masculine trap of wanting to enclose us in our differences."[18]

Conflict And Consensus

Fierce debate surrounds the importance or otherwise of de Beauvoir's ideas, but *The Second Sex* had a clear impact on mainstream readers. Thousands of French women were influenced by reading the book in secret before the 1970s,[19] while the public view of *The Second Sex* shifted in line with the radical movements and civil unrest of the 1960s. French factory workers demanded better conditions, ethnic minorities fought institutional racism,* and in 1968 the women's rights movement* was born.

This is where the arguments start.Toril Moi has written extensively on French feminism's disregard for *The Second Sex*. She interprets this as springing from a rejection of existentialist thought that casts de Beauvoir as a "theoretical dinosaur."[20] Catherine Rodgers,* however, says Moi does not acknowledge de Beauvoir's influence on French egalitarian feminists, and even de Beauvoir failed to recognize her own legacy.[21] Rodgers argues that leaders of the *Mouvement de libération des femmes** would certainly have read *The Second Sex*. She puts the book's absence from feminist writings of the era down to the fact that its arguments had become commonplace.[22]

De Beauvoir claimed that second-wave feminists* in France (1960s to late 1980s) "may have become feminists for the reasons that I explain in *The Second Sex*, but they discovered those reasons in their life experiences, not in my book." [23] Scholars continue to debate whether she is right.

NOTES

1   Ursula Tidd, *Simone de Beauvoir* (London: Routledge, 2004), 101.

2   As cited in Sylvie Chaperon, *Les années Beauvoir: 1945–1970 (The Beauvoir Years: 1945–1970)* (Paris: Fayard, 2000), 182; and Margaret A. Simons, "Introduction," in *Simone de Beauvoir: Feminist Writings*, ed. Margaret A. Simons and Marybeth Timmermann (Chicago: University of Illinois Press, 2015), 4–5.

3   As cited in Chaperon, *Les années Beauvoir,* 175–7.

4   Tidd, *Simone de Beauvoir*, 101.

5   Simone de Beauvoir, *Lettres à Sartre (Letters to Sartre)*, ed. Sylvie le Bon (Paris: Gallimard, 1990), Vol. II, 284, as cited in Margaret A. Simons, "*The Second Sex*: From Marxism to Radical Feminism," in *Feminist Interpretations of Simone de Beauvoir,* ed. Margaret A. Simons (University Park, PA: Pennsylvania State University Press, 1995), 2.

6   Toril Moi, *Simone de Beauvoir: The Making of an Intellectual Woman* (New York: Oxford University Press, 1994), 98.

7   Eric Berkowitz, *Sex and Punishment: Four Thousand Years of Judging Desire* (Berkeley, CA: Counterpoint, 2012).

8   Jean-Raymond Audet, *Simone de Beauvoir face à la morte* (Lausanne: Éditions L'Age de L'Homme, 1979), 122–5.

9   Michèle Le Doeuff, *Hipparchia's Choice*, trans. Trista Selous (New York: Columbia University Press, 1990).

10 Moi, *Simone de Beauvoir*, 96.

11 Moi, *Simone de Beauvoir*, 98.

12 Moi, *Simone de Beauvoir*, 101.

13 Tidd, *Simone de Beauvoir*, 102.

14 Tidd, *Simone de Beauvoir*, 102.

15 Jean-Louis Servan-Schreiber, "Why I Am a Feminist: Interview with Simone de Beauvoir [1975]," accessed March 5, 2015, www.youtube.com/watch?v=v2LkME3MMNk.

16 Margaret A. Simons, "*The Second Sex*: From Marxism to Radical Feminism," in *Feminist Interpretations of Simone de Beauvoir,* ed. Margaret A. Simons (University Park: Pennsylvania State University Press, 1995), 260.

17 John Gerassi, "Interview with Simone de Beauvoir: *The Second Sex*, 25 Years Later," *Society* (January–February 1976), accessed May 5, 2015, www.marxists.org/reference/subject/ethics/de-beauvoir/1976/interview.htm.

18 Margaret A. Simons and Jessica Benjamin, "Beauvoir Interview (1979)," in *Beauvoir and the Second Sex*, ed. Margaret A. Simons (New York: Rowman & Littlefield), 19.

19 Catherine Rodgers, "The Influence of *The Second Sex* on the French Feminist Scene," in *Simone de Beauvoir's* The Second Sex*: New Interdisciplinary* Essays, ed. Ruth Evans (Manchester: Manchester University Press, 1998), 64.

20 Moi, *Simone de Beauvoir*, 98.

21 Rodgers, "The Influence of *The Second Sex*," 67.

22 Rodgers, "The Influence of *The Second Sex*," 64.

23 Gerassi, "Interview with Simone de Beauvoir."

MODULE 10
THE EVOLVING DEBATE

KEY POINTS

- There have been many different views as to what de Beauvoir meant when defining gender.

- De Beauvoir's work helped to create room in academic scholarship for women's studies* and gender studies.*

- People read *The Second Sex* today to gain insight into a number of different things, from gender and identity to how socio-economic regimes can affect oppression.

Uses And Problems

Simone de Beauvoir's *The Second Sex* remains controversial, not least because it opens up whole new areas of enquiry. Elisabeth Spelman* argues that de Beauvoir's work is undermined by concentrating on the oppression of white, middle-class women.[1] Judith Okely,* on the other hand, does not see this as a problem. She says this limited focus offers an opportunity to examine de Beauvoir as a case study, because her work provides insight into the lives of an entire generation of such women in France.

Scholars are also at odds over how useful and accurate de Beauvoir's definition of gender as a social construct* really is. Sociology,* psychology,* and gender studies have all accepted her assertion that identity cannot simply be reduced to anatomy, to the body we are born in. Yet academics have tended to read *The Second Sex* as explicitly denying there is any actual difference between the genders.

Debra Bergoffen* and Moira Gatens have challenged this approach.[2] Both argue that de Beauvoir's understanding of the relationship between the concepts of "feminine," "woman," and

> ❝ Feminine voices are silent when it comes to concrete action ... the true control of the world has never been in the hands of women; they have not brought their influence to bear upon technique or economy, they have not made and unmade states, they have not discovered new worlds. Through them certain events have been set off, but the women have been pretexts rather than agents. ❞
>
> Simone de Beauvoir, *The Second Sex*

"female" is more complicated than just sex versus gender. This suggests de Beauvoir is far more radical than critics understand.[3] Such new readings continue to shed fresh light on *The Second Sex* as part of contemporary gender studies.

Schools Of Thought

The Second Sex is integral to feminism* because it pioneered the public discussion of female sexuality. As Elizabeth Badinter* puts it, de Beauvoir's "message ... was heard by my whole generation."[4]

In the United States and Canada, de Beauvoir inspired the creation of centers for women's studies from the 1970s onwards.[5] Her ideas also played an important role in the sociology of gender, which emerged in the mid-1950s to address how masculinity and femininity are perceived and whether gender is a result of our anatomy or whether it is imposed by our upbringing. The 1970s saw the development of feminist approaches to the sociology of gender, which increasingly used de Beauvoir's argument that gender is a product of culture. In the 1990s gender studies emerged to tackle the perception of gender across culture, including literature, film, and visual art. Gender theorists explore the effects of socialization* on gender and their work is heavily indebted to de Beauvoir.

Within the traditional male-dominated field of philosophy* Janna

Thompson* and Dorothy E. Smith* used de Beauvoir's existentialist* feminism to introduce a female perspective. Thompson's edited collection of essays *Women and Philosophy* (1976) explores how philosophy might aid women's emancipation.* She investigates concepts such as individualism, identity, androgyny (the combination of feminine and masculine characteristics), and free will. The essays ask how much a woman's identity is limited by patriarchal* values and whether (in contrast to de Beauvoir's assertion) it can develop independently.[6]

Smith's book, *The Everyday World as Problematic: A Feminist Sociology* (1987), explores the difficulties in developing a feminist sociology. The question "What is a woman?" reminds us that humankind is viewed in male terms. So in the same way, the question "What is feminist sociology?" reminds us that this field is shaped by male interests and views.[7] *The Everyday World as Problematic* marked an important step in challenging feminist scholarship, warning how feminism might end up marginalizing women further.

In Current Scholarship

The Second Sex continues to be read by different people for different reasons. Gender theorists such as Judith Butler* and Moira Gatens see de Beauvoir's work as part of a wider debate about whether gender is inborn or imposed, and whether a woman can forge her own identity despite her condition as "Other."*

Feminist historians and Marxist* thinkers read the book primarily for insights into the role of different socio-economic regimes (particularly capitalism*) in female oppression. For Mary Spongber's* *Writing Women's History since the Renaissance* (2002), de Beauvoir's ideas are the key to explaining women's perceived absence from history.[8]

The Second Sex is often referenced in introductions to feminist theory, both as a milestone in feminist thought and as an important female perspective on the human sciences. Andrea Nye's* *Feminist*

Theory and the Philosophies of Man (2013) pays tribute to the enduring relevance of de Beauvoir's ideas as patriarchal values continue to overshadow philosophical thought and literary interpretations.[9]

Philosophers have an abiding interest in how writer and philosopher Jean-Paul Sartre* influenced de Beauvoir's work. At first it was assumed *The Second Sex* had been shaped by his ideas, leading some to challenge its originality or even to label it self-contradictory. How could a feminist base her work on a philosophy so steeped in Sartre's well-documented misogyny?*[10] But Bergoffen and Christine Daigle* use de Beauvoir's diaries to prove that her ideas pre-dated her relationship with Sartre. It was actually de Beauvoir who influenced *his* work.[11] This debate resulted in *Sartre and Beauvoir: Questions of Influence* (2009), a collection of essays by leading de Beauvoir scholars. They considered how assumptions about Sartre's influence might well have affected the critical reception of *The Second Sex*.[12]

NOTES

1   Elisabeth Spelman, *Inessential Woman: Problems of Exclusion in Feminist Thought* (Boston: Beacon Press, 1988), 63–4.

2   Debra Bergoffen, "(Re)counting the Sexual Difference," and Moira Gatens, "De Beauvoir and Biology: A Second Look," in *The Cambridge Companion to Simone de Beauvoir,* ed. Claudia Card (Cambridge: Cambridge University Press, 2003), 248–65 and 266–85, respectively.

3   Gatens, "De Beauvoir and Biology," 267; Bergoffen, "(Re)counting the Sexual Difference," 250.

4   Catherine Rodgers, "The Influence of *The Second Sex* on the French Feminist Scene," in *Simone de Beauvoir's* The Second Sex*: New Interdisciplinary* Essays, ed. Ruth Evans (Manchester: Manchester University Press, 1998), 67.

5   Lisa Appignanesi, *Simone de Beauvoir* (London: Haus, 2005), 160.

6   Janna Thompson, *Women and Philosophy* (Bundoora: Australasian Association of Philosophy, 1986).

7   Dorothy E. Smith, *The Everyday World as Problematic: A Feminist Sociology* (Boston: Northeastern University Press, 1987).

8   Mary Spongber, *Writing Women's History since the Renaissance* (New York: Palgrave Macmillan, 2002).

9   Andrea Nye, *Feminist Theory and the Philosophies of Man* (London: Routledge, 2013).

10   Margery Collins and Christine Pierce, "Holes and Slime: Sexism in Sartre's Psychoanalysis," in *Women and Philosophy*, ed. Carol C. Gould and Marx W. Wartofsky (New York: Capricorn Books, 1976).

11   Margaret A. Simons, "Is *The Second Sex* Beauvoir's Application of Sartrean Existentialism?" paper given at the Twentieth World Congress of Philosophy, Boston, MA, August 10–15, 1998; Edward Fullbrook and Kate Fullbrook, *Sex and Philosophy: Re-thinking de Beauvoir and Sartre* (London: Bloomsbury, 2008).

12   Christine Daigle and Jacob Golomb, eds, *Sartre and Beauvoir: The Question of Influence*, (Bloomington: Indiana University Press, 2009).

MODULE 11
IMPACT AND INFLUENCE TODAY

KEY POINTS

- Many contemporary feminists* argue that modern society's attitudes to women have not changed all that much since de Beauvoir wrote *The Second Sex.*

- Issues of gender and how modern life still wants to construct ideas of what a woman is from a very early age remain topics that arouse passionate feelings on both sides.

- Questions still remain about whether English translations of *The Second Sex* have clouded de Beauvoir's original arguments.

Position

It is difficult to imagine a branch of feminist thought that is not influenced by Simone de Beauvoir's *The Second Sex* as either an inspiration or a source of argument. Feminism has evolved considerably since the book appeared in 1949, but many claims made by contemporary feminists are rooted in its ideas.

Natasha Walters's* *Living Dolls: The Return of Sexism* (2010) takes its title from de Beauvoir's description of women as "marvelous doll[s]."[1] Walters uses *The Second Sex* to argue that Western society has actually changed very little since de Beauvoir's day. She examines developments over the last half-century to show that the effects of post-1960 second-wave feminism were short-lived. Female emancipation* has become synonymous with the right to dress seductively and have casual sex rather than gaining an equal footing in the workplace or politics.

> **❝** It was the social regime founded on private property that entailed the guardianship of the married woman, and it is the technological evolution accomplished by men that has emancipated the women of today. **❞**
>
> Simone de Beauvoir, *The Second Sex*

Walters echoes the fears de Beauvoir expressed in *The Second Sex*, that it is all too easy for feminism to be folded back into a patriarchal* narrative.[2] So when members of the Russian feminist group Pussy Riot* go topless to protest as a shock tactic, they are actually playing into the male gaze. Pussy Riot's message goes unheard as onlookers focus instead on their breasts.

De Beauvoir's ideas also informed the seminal 1990 work by Judith Butler,* *Gender Trouble*.[3] Butler wants to know how gender identity and sexuality are defined and agrees with de Beauvoir that gender is not biological, but is imposed by culture and society. However, where de Beauvoir argues that patriarchal society views women as a lack or an absence, Butler argues there is no such thing as gender in the first place. Even the distinction between male and female genitalia is false because our understanding is based on social norms. This is to say that our understanding of the difference between male and female genitalia and their connotations is, itself, socially constructed. Butler's controversial text develops de Beauvoir's ideas in important new ways, making us reconsider our understanding of biology and gender.

Interaction

Machiavelli's work did not give rise to a defined school of thought. De Beauvoir's work remains relevant to the public debate, from how girls are told to wear pink to sexism* in the online gaming world. Campaigns to challenge gender bias in children's clothes and toys, for example, include Pinkstinks. Their campaign highlights how toys primarily emphasizing appearance, fashion, and shopping have a damaging effect, severely limiting girls' aspirations. These ideas chime with Peggy Orenstein's and Rebecca Hains's respective books, *Cinderella Ate My Daughter* (2011) and *The Princess Problem* (2014), which tackle how the market divides into "for boys" and "for girls" to increase profits at the expense of children.[4]

Like de Beauvoir, contemporary feminists often face intense criticism. The founders of Pinkstinks receive hate mail from around the world. Laura Bates's* Everyday Sexism Twitter campaign (http://everydaysexism.com/) invites women to share their experiences of sexual discrimination. She was slated by men's rights groups, who argued that the project exaggerated the extent of sexism in society. In 2014, critics of misogyny* (dislike or hatred of women) in the video games industry received hundreds of death threats in a vitriolic campaign that made global headlines. "Gamergate" reflected ongoing issues about how women are represented in popular culture. Meanwhile, Caroline Criado-Perez's 2014 campaign for a woman to appear on UK banknotes resulted in Jane Austen being selected for the £10 note—but also in Criado-Perez receiving death threats on Twitter.

These intense reactions suggest that attitudes to gender identity and sexuality cause feeling to run every bit as high today as when *The Second Sex* first appeared. They show that the project de Beauvoir began is not yet finished. If anything, the anonymity afforded by social media has ushered in a new set of challenges for feminist activists campaigning in the digital arena. The potential for online harassment, stalking, and abuse risks turning the Internet into one further space in which women's actions are curtailed, and their views silenced.

The Continuing Debate

The Second Sex is central to the academic disciplines of gender studies,* queer studies,* and feminist criticism. For contemporary scholars,

The Second Sex remains interesting for its historical, global impact. The work was again in the spotlight in 1983 when the feminist critic Margaret Simons* published an important essay, "The Silencing of Simone de Beauvoir." Simons laid out in minute detail the discrepancies between the original French text and the English translation by H. M. Parshley.* He left out between a tenth and a third of the text and was a zoologist with no background in either philosophy* or history. Simons argued that Parshley was not qualified for the job and mistranslated several of the book's central philosophical concepts. He effectively undermined de Beauvoir's feminist argument by translating it into male-oriented terms. For instance, he translated "humanité" as "mankind" rather than "humankind," and "le soi" as "man" rather than "self."

Simons' revelations led some scholars to question whether previous assessments of the book based on Parshley's translation could even be trusted.[5] A new English translation was published in 2009 and an extended version followed in 2012, but again these raised new questions. Feminist writer Toril Moi,* who argued that the true meaning of de Beauvoir's existentialist* argument is skewed by the book's first translation, was appalled by the new version. She claimed it suffered many errors of omission, syntax, and mistranslation.[6]

NOTES

1   Simone de Beauvoir, *The Second Sex*, trans. H. M. Parshley (New York: Alfred A. Knopf, 1953), 304.

2   Natasha Walters, *Living Dolls: The Return of Sexism* (London: Virago, 2010), 129.

3   Judith Butler, "Sex and Gender in Simone de Beauvoir's Second Sex," *Yale French Studies* 72 (1986): 35–49, and *Gender Trouble: Feminism and the Subversion of Identity* (London: Routledge, 1990), 11, 13, 190.

4   Peggy Orenstein, *Cinderella Ate My Daughter: Dispatches from the Front Lines of the New Girlie-Girl Culture* (New York: Harper, 2011); Rebecca Hains, *The Princess Problem: Guiding Our Girls through the Princess-obsessed Years* (Naperville, IL: Sourcebooks, 2014).

5   Margaret A. Simons, "The Silencing of Simone de Beauvoir," *Women's Studies International Forum* 6, no. 6 (1983): 559–664.

6   Toril Moi, "The Adulteress Wife," *London Review of Books* 32, no. 3 (February 11, 2010), accessed February 2, 2015, www.lrb.co.uk/v32/n03/toril-moi/the-adulteress-wife.

WHERE NEXT?

KEY POINTS

- Simone de Beauvoir's *The Second Sex* is still inspiring people to think and write about gender, identity, and feminism* today.

- People are applying de Beauvoir's ideas to interesting new areas, including political science.*

- The impact of *The Second Sex* on modern society and its attitude to women is both huge and undeniable.

Potential

Simone de Beauvoir's claim in *The Second Sex* that "one is not born, but rather becomes a woman"[1] was a rallying cry for feminist activists in the 1970s. Today it is still a powerful idea in discussions about the origins of gender identity and sexual orientation. Some of de Beauvoir's ideas that were radical at the time—that women should be able to work or choose not to have children—are now accepted in Western culture. Likewise, she has been proved right by the discrediting of psychoanalytic* concepts such as "penis envy,"* by both psychologists* and feminist theorists, who have found little basis for it. Indeed, the theory itself has led many feminists to distance themselves from psychoanalysis as a whole, seeing the theory as representative of the discipline's deep-rooted misogyny.*

However, *The Second Sex* still has a lot to offer contemporary discussions about gender and sexuality. *The Second Sex* may prove more useful to twenty-first-century feminists than those in the 1970s and 1980s. The emergence of queer theory* and gender studies* brings new attention to de Beauvoir because they also question the ways we

> **❝**The period in which we live is a period in transition; this world, which has always belonged to the men, is still in their hands: the institutions and the values of the patriarchal civilization still survive in large part. **❞**
>
> Simone de Beauvoir, *The Second Sex*

define gender and sexual orientation. Her central argument that femininity is a tool of ideological oppression and that womanhood itself is a social construct* has gained new relevance.

Mariam Motamedi-Fraser's* *Identity Without Selfhood: Simone de Beauvoir and Bisexuality* (1999) is one example of how of de Beauvoir's theories are part of contemporary discussions about gender.[2] Motamedi-Fraser examines biographical, media, and academic accounts of de Beauvoir to show the impact of Western ideas about identity and sexuality on scholarly interpretations of her work. Motamedi-Fraser suggests that de Beauvoir's sexual relationships and her writing on sexuality are more complex and subtle than scholars have assumed. The book considers how cultural understandings of sexual orientation in turn shape and inform scholarship—and can lead to misinterpretation.

Toril Moi's* *Simone de Beauvoir: The Making of an Intellectual Woman* (1993) and *What Is a Woman?* (1999) examine de Beauvoir's views on femininity in relation to the whole feminist movement and show how competing theories obscured de Beauvoir's ideas for decades.[3] Margaret Simons's* book-length study *Beauvoir and the Second Sex: Feminism, Race and the Origins of Existentialism* (1999) opened up the discussion on links between feminism, anti-colonialism,* and human rights activism.[4] There is potential for more applications of de Beauvoir's work in discussions about women's rights* in the developing world. Echoing de Beauvoir's assertion that patriarchal* societies view women as "not-men," Sharmon Lynette Monogan* writes compellingly about the role that patriarchal values play in the tradition of female genital mutilation.*[5]

Future Directions

Elizabeth Fallaize,* Toril Moi, and Margaret Simons are de Beauvoir's most vocal champions and their work examines her impact within the history of feminist thought and also within the existentialist* tradition. They have been joined more recently by Ruth Evans,* Eleanor Holveck, Ursula Tidd, Sonia Kruks, and Emily Grosholz, who have all helped to increase de Beauvoir's visibility in the humanities and social sciences.

Holveck's *Simone de Beauvoir's Philosophy of Lived Experience* (2002) examines de Beauvoir's existentialist thought across her fiction and philosophy.* The book takes a fresh approach to *The Second Sex* by relating it to the philosophical essays de Beauvoir wrote earlier in her career.[6] Tidd's *Simone de Beauvoir* (2004) provides fresh readings of all of de Beauvoir's works.[7] Grosholz's *The Legacy of Simone de Beauvoir* (2006) addresses the influence of de Beauvoir on later feminist thought.[8] Kruks's *Simone de Beauvoir and the Politics of Ambiguity* (2012) applies her work to the field of political science—a little-explored area that Kruks finds fruitful in discussing women's role in politics.[9] Each of these texts is testament to the enduring relevance of de Beauvoir's book and the scope for new interpretations in light of the cultural shifts that followed.

Summary

The Second Sex is an important investigation into women's oppression throughout history, and a pivotal moment in the emancipation* of women. De Beauvoir shows us exactly how sexism* has seeped into modern society and how it evolved throughout the ages to ensure that women remain submissive. Through her explanation and investigation of popular ideas about femininity, as well as her analysis of women's social and economic dependence on men, de Beauvoir paved the way for the second wave of feminism during the sexual revolution* of the 1960s and into the 1970s. Her work is also used today in discussions about gender identity and sexual orientation.

A twenty-first-century reader might view de Beauvoir's ideas as old fashioned or obvious. But even if some of de Beauvoir's calls to action seem dated (that women should work, for example), the work itself remains intensely relevant. Her analysis remains powerful for its examination of the impact of cultural myths,* the effect of ideas about femininity on child development, and her challenge to traditional definitions of gender and sexuality.

Of course, *The Second Sex* stands out for its historical importance. This is the book that launched the women's rights movement in France. De Beauvoir helped bring about the sexual revolution and feminism as we know it today. As Elizabeth Badinter* commented in her epitaph to de Beauvoir, "Women, you owe everything to her!"[10]

NOTES

1   Simone de Beauvoir, *The Second Sex*, trans. H. M. Parshley (New York: Alfred A. Knopf, 1953), 249.

2   Mariam Motamedi-Fraser, *Identity Without Selfhood: Simone de Beauvoir and Bisexuality* (Cambridge: Cambridge University Press, 1999).

3   Toril Moi, *Simone de Beauvoir: The Making of an Intellectual Woman* (Oxford and New York: Oxford University Press, 1993); *What Is a Woman?* (Oxford and New York: Oxford University Press, 1999).

4   Margaret A. Simons, *Beauvoir and the Second Sex: Feminism, Race and the Origins of Existentialism* (Lanham, MD, and Oxford: Rowman & Littlefield, 1999).

5   Sharmon Lynette Monogan, "Patriarchy: Perpetuating the Practice of Female Genital Mutilation," *International Research Journal of Arts & Humanities* 37 (2010): 83–99.

6   Eleanore Holveck, *Simone de Beauvoir's Philosophy of Lived Experience* (New York: Rowman & Littlefield, 2002).

7   Ursula Tidd, *Simone de Beauvoir* (London: Routledge, 2004).

8   Emily Grosholz, *The Legacy of Simone de Beauvoir* (Oxford: Oxford University Press, 2006).

9   Sonia Kruks, *Simone de Beauvoir and the Politics of Ambiguity* (Oxford: Oxford University Press, 2012).

10 As cited in Deirdre Bair, *Simone de Beauvoir: A Biography* (London: Cape, 1991), 617.

GLOSSARY

GLOSSARY OF TERMS

Alienation: an individual's estrangement from his or her community. It is often referred to in relation to Karl Marx's theory of social alienation, which argued that alienation is a consequence of the unequal distribution of wealth and power.

American Civil Rights movement: a movement in the United States to secure equal rights for black people, extending to outlawing segregation and removing current discriminatory legislation against blacks. The movement gained sway in the mid-1950s but was at its most intense in the 1960s.

Anthropology: the study of humans and human behavior, and their cultures. The field draws on a number of others disciplines in the physical, biological, social, and human sciences.

Anti-colonialism: the critique of or opposition to the system of colonialism and colonial rule, either by the colonized or by external parties who view the system as socially or economical unjust.

Anti-Semitism: prejudice against, fear of, and discrimination against Jewish people based on their ethnicity, beliefs, and/or heritage.

Autonomy: the independence and freedom of either action or belief. An autonomous individual is one who can believe and act as s/he wishes.

Bluestocking: a term used to describe an educated, intellectual woman. It originated in the eighteenth century, but acquired negative connotations in the following century, becoming a term for a frumpy or unattractive bookish woman.

Bourgeois: a term used in Marxist theory to refer to the wealthy class, which owns the means of production (for example, the owner of a shop, a factory, or any other entity that produces goods or services).

Capitalism: a mode of production and an economic system in which industries, trade, and the means of production are either largely or entirely privately owned, and in which production and trade are done for profit.

Colonialism: the rule of one country by another, involving unequal power relations between the rulers (colonists) and ruled (colonies), and the exploitation of the colonies' resources to strengthen the economy of the colonizers' home countries.

Dehumanization: the systematic process of demonizing another person or persons by making them appear less than human, and therefore not deserving of humane treatment.

Differential feminism: a strand of feminism that argues the need to recognize that men and women are different, and that seeks to celebrate the different attributes that women offer. For differential feminists, gender equality should not be based on the assumption that women behave like men.

Dowry: the goods, cash, or property that a bride's family gives to the bridegroom in exchange for agreeing to support her and any children they may have.

Egalitarianism: the championing of equal treatment, based on the assumption that all humans are equal in worth and social status.

Emancipation: the procurement of social, economic, and/or political rights or equality by a previously disenfranchised group.

Existentialism/existential humanism: a branch of philosophy that places emphasis on the human subject's struggle for self-understanding, self-knowledge, and responsibility in the absence of a god.

Female genital mutilation (FGM): the ritual cutting or removal of some or all of the external female genitalia, which is designed to control women's sexuality by either denying them sexual pleasure, or preserving their virginity before marriage.

Feminism: a series of ideologies and movements concerned with equal social, political, cultural, and economic rights for women, including equal rights in the home, workplace, education, and government.

French Resistance: a term used to describe those who opposed the Vichy regime that collaborated with the Nazis in occupied France during World War II. Members of the Resistance published an underground newspaper, provided first-hand intelligence to the Allies, and participated in guerrilla welfare.

Gay rights movement: refers to a series of events, including public protests, lobbying, and demonstrations from the 1970s to the present day, through which homosexual men and women sought to redress the stigma of homosexuality and attain equal rights to heterosexuals, including the right to marry and to have children.

Gender relations: any interaction between the two genders based on the social roles designated to each one.

Gender studies: the interdisciplinary academic study of gender relations, gender identity, and sexual orientation, including how gender and sexual orientation are perceived and/or represented in culture.

Hegelian dialectics: a form of philosophical discussion that involves putting forth one's argument (thesis), providing the counterargument (antithesis), and then reaching a conclusion (synthesis) that seeks to reconcile the two.

Historical materialism: an approach to historical criticism developed by Karl Marx, which examines history in relation to class relations and income inequality.

Index of Forbidden Books: a list of books banned by the Roman Catholic Church due to allegedly improper content, often regarding sexuality or social behavior that goes against the dictates of the Church.

Ingénue: a French word for innocent, often used to describe a sheltered, naïve, or sexually inexperienced female.

Interdisciplinarity: the study of a problem, question, or topic that combines different disciplines, schools of thought, or theoretical approaches.

Jewish: an ethno-cultural and ethno-religious group that originated in the Ancient Middle East from the Israelites.

Lacanian psychoanalysis: a branch of psychoanalysis founded by Jacques Lacan that examines the development of identity from early childhood.

Literary criticism: the evaluation, study, and interpretation of literature.

Malagasy Uprising (1947–8): a nationalist rebellion against French rule in the French colony of Madagascar. The uprising was violently repressed by the French military, which carried our mass executions, torture, and war rape of the country's inhabitants.

Marxism: refers to cultural, philosophical, socio-economic, political, and aesthetic readings based on the work of the nineteenth-century political economist Karl Marx. Marxist theorists and writers are concerned with the growth of social inequality under capitalism, and the influence this has on culture and society.

Matrilineal descent or **matrilineality:** a form of hereditary succession that sees the individual as a descendant of his/her mother's family. This pattern contrasts with the more common pattern of patrilineage, which traces descent through the father's family.

Misogyny: the dislike or hatred of women, and behavior that reflects that hatred, including sexual discrimination against women, violence, denigration, and the treatment of women as passive objects (also known as objectification).

Mouvement de libération des femmes **(Women's Liberation Movement):** the first women's rights movement in France, founded in 1968, which sought to attain the right to contraception, abortion, and equal rights in the workplace.

Myth or **cultural myth:** beliefs born out of a culture's ideology, faith, or world-view.

Narcissism: excessive self-absorption or interest in one's own self.

Nazis: also known as the National Socialist Party, they ruled in Germany from 1933 to the end of World War II in 1945, a period known as the Third Reich. Nazi ideology was essentially fascist, and incorporated anti-Semitism and scientific racism.

Négritude: a literary movement running from the 1930s to the late 1950s, begun by Afro-Caribbean writers living in Paris to protest against French colonial rule and French cultural assimilation.

Objectification: a philosophical term that refers to any instance in which a person is treated as a thing. The term "female objectification" is commonly used in discussions on gender to refer to the treatment of women as objects without agency or purpose other than attracting, or being attractive to, men.

Obsolescence: an object, idea, or person's passage into disuse or irrelevance due to the passing of time.

Other: the term philosophers use for that which is separate or distinct from the human self.

Patriarchy or **patriarchal society:** refers to any social system in which men hold the most power, often in roles of political leadership, are granted privilege in the control of property, hold moral authority, or are granted authority over female relatives and children.

Penis envy: a term used by psychoanalysts until the mid-1950s. According to this theory, females' transition from childhood to adulthood involves the realization that men have penises and that they do not.

Philosophy: a field of the humanities that studies fundamental human problems related to reality, knowledge, existence, reason, language, and values.

Political science: a field of the social sciences that examines government policies and politics, and the dynamics of nation, government, and state.

Proletarian: in Marxist theory, this is the term used to define the working class, which earns money by working for the bourgeoisie.

Psychoanalysis: a discipline founded by the Austrian physician Sigmund Freud, which explores the unconscious workings of the human mind and considers the role of repression and desire in human development.

Psychology: an academic and applied discipline concerning the study and treatment of mental behavior and mental functions.

Queer theory: an approach to critical theory that questions or rejects traditional ideas of sexuality or gender identity in literary and cultural subjects.

Racism: refers to both discrimination and prejudice based on the perception of biological differences between people, including race and ethnicity.

Roman Catholic Church: the largest Christian Church, and among the oldest religious institutions in the world. Its doctrines include the outlawing of abortion and any contraception beyond natural family planning.

Second-wave feminism: refers to the women's rights movement from the 1960s, coinciding with the sexual revolution and lasting up until the late 1980s. In contrast to first-wave feminism, women at this time were fighting for sexual emancipation, the legalization of abortion, and equal pay in the workplace.

Sexism: discrimination or prejudice based on a person's gender. This might include treating a person as an inferior, or making assumptions about them due to their gender.

Sexology: the study of human sexuality, including sexual interests, functions, and behavior.

Sexual revolution: a systematic dismantling of traditional social codes and mores regarding sexuality and sexual propriety that took place throughout the United States and Europe from 1960 to 1980. This included the normalization of premarital sex and of the use of contraception, and the legalization of abortion in many countries.

Social construct: any category or definition used by society to group people together or define them. Social constructs are often used to privilege a particular group over others, for instance men over women, or one race over another.

Socialist revolution: refers to the overthrow of capitalism and the introduction of a socialist government, which would effect structural changes in society, including the redistribution of wealth and the eradication of social inequality.

Socialization: the processes by which human beings learn from others, including but not limited to how they absorb systems of belief, learn particular modes of behavior, and develop views about gender, race, or sexuality.

Sociology: the academic study of social behavior. The discipline examines the origins and development of social relations, their different modes of organization, and different social institutions.

Soviet Union: a single-party Marxist-Leninist state comprising 15 socialist republics in Eastern Europe, including Russia, Georgia, and the Ukraine, that existed between 1922 and 1991.

Subjugation: conquering and gaining control of someone or something and rendering them subordinate.

Suffragette: a term used to describe women in the late nineteenth and early twentieth centuries who fought for the right to vote.

***The Taming of the Shrew* (1590–3):** a play by William Shakespeare, which describes a man's systematic domestication of a rebellious, strong-minded woman (the "shrew" of the title).

***Les Temps Modernes*:** a left-wing journal founded by Jean-Paul Sartre and Simone de Beauvoir in 1945, named after Charlie Chaplin's film *Modern Times*.

United Nations: an intergovernmental organization, established in 1945, to promote cooperation between nations.

Vichy regime (1940–4): a provisional government installed in France during World War II after France surrendered to Nazi Germany, and which collaborated with the Nazis.

Women and Socialism: a written history of female oppression from prehistoric times to the end of the nineteenth century. Its author, the German socialist August Bebel, argued that women's emancipation was key to the success of socialism.

Women's rights movement: a series of efforts to attain rights for women equal to those of men. The movement occurred in stages, and rights were gained at different times in different countries. However, it is generally recognized as having reached its height in the late 1960s and early 1970s.

Women's studies: the interdisciplinary study of gender, sexuality, class, race, and nationhood, which addresses female identity as a combination of these factors. The discipline emerged in the United States in the 1970s and was strongly influenced by second-wave feminism.

World War II (1939–45): a war fought between Britain, France, the Soviet Union, the United States, and others against Germany, Italy, and Japan.v

PEOPLE MENTIONED IN THE TEXT

Elizabeth Badinter (b. 1944) is a French historian, writer, and professor of philosophy at Paris's École Polytechnique. She is known for her feminist writings, which include the controversial *Conflict, Women, Motherhood* (2010).

Johann Bachoffen (1815–87) was a German anthropologist and writer best known for his argument that prehistoric and early modern societies were matriarchal—that is, they gave more power to women.

Laura Bates is a British feminist activist and journalist best known for her Everyday Sexism campaign, which seeks to raise awareness of the sexism women experience on a daily basis.

August Bebel (1840–1913) was a German socialist writer and politician. He is best known for his book *Women and Socialism* (1879).

Debra Bergoffen is the Bishop Hamilton Lecturer in Philosophy at American University and Professor Emerita of Philosophy at George Mason University. She writes on contemporary philosophical thought, feminist theory, and human rights.

André Breton (1896–1966) was a French writer, poet, and visual artist, and one of the founders of Surrealism, a radical artistic movement in the early twentieth century. He is perhaps best known for his novels *Nadja* (1928) and *Mad Love* (1937).

Judith Butler (b. 1956) is a feminist and scholar of queer theory and gender relations best known for her book *Gender Trouble* (1990), in which she argues that gender is purely a social construct entirely separate from biological or anatomical facts.

Albert Camus (1913–60) was a French novelist, playwright, existentialist philosopher, and journalist, and was awarded the Nobel Prize for Literature in 1957.

Hélène Cixous (b. 1937) is a French feminist poet, philosopher, and literary critic, best known for her feminist book *The Laugh of the Medusa* (1975), which urges female readers to escape the phallocentrism (penis-centered nature) of modern language and adopt what she calls "female writing" (écriture féminine).

Paul Claudel (1868–1955) was a French poet and playwright whose work de Beauvoir criticizes intensely in *The Second Sex* for its misogynistic depiction of women.

Caroline Criado-Perez (b. 1984) is an English journalist and feminist activist known for her efforts to allow women better representation in the British media, and to be depicted on banknotes. This last campaign resulted in the Bank of England's decision to put Jane Austen on the £10 banknote by 2017.

Christine Daigle is professor of philosophy at Brock University in California, specializing in existentialism, phenomenology, and feminist theory in the continental tradition.

Friedrich Engels (1820–95) was a German philosopher and close colleague of Karl Marx, with whom he wrote *The Communist Manifesto* (1848). His book *The Origins of the Family, Private Property and the State* (1884) inspired many of de Beauvoir's ideas, and is now considered an important text by feminist scholars.

Ruth Evans is Dorothy McBride Orthwein Professor at Saint Louis University in Missouri, specializing in Middle English literature (1300–1580) and feminist theory and criticism.

Elizabeth Fallaize (1950–2009) was a British academic, feminist, leading figure in French studies, and international authority on the work of Simone de Beauvoir, including both her novels and philosophical writings.

Antoinette Fouque (1936–2014) was a French psychoanalyst and feminist activist who co-founded France's women's rights movement, the *Mouvement de libération des femmes*, in 1968. She is recognized as one of the country's most pre-eminent feminists.

Kate Fullbrook (1951–2003) was an American-born academic best known for campaigning in the UK for the right to a liberal education, and for her writings on feminist theory, modernist fiction by women, and Simone de Beauvoir's relationship with Sartre.

Georg Wilhem Friedrich Hegel (1770–1831) was a German philosopher and a major figure in the Idealism movement. He became well known for his historicist and realist accounts of reality. His concept of a "system" of integration between mind and nature, subject and object, and so on, was one of the first conceptual moves that acknowledged contradictions and oppositions within such a system.

Luce Irigaray (b. 1930) is a Belgian-born French feminist philosopher, linguist, and cultural theorist best known for *Speculum of the Other Woman* (1974) and *This Sex Which Is Not One* (1977).

Fiona Jenkins is a senior lecturer in the School of Philosophy at the Australian National University, specializing in contemporary French philosophy.

Alfred Kinsey (1894–1956) was an American biologist and professor of zoology best remembered for his pioneering work in the field of sexology, which he recounted in the books *Sexual Behavior in the Human Male* (1948) and *Sexual Behavior in the Human Female* (1953).

Julia Kristeva (b. 1941) is a Bulgarian French feminist philosopher, psychoanalyst, and literary critic best known for her books *Powers of Horror* (1982), *Woman's Time* (1981), and *Black Sun* (1992).

Jacques Lacan (1901–81) was a French psychoanalyst and psychiatrist best known for his development of Lacanian psychoanalysis, which had a profound influence on French philosophy and feminist theory.

D. H. Lawrence (1885–1930) was a British novelist, short-story writer, and essayist best known for his novel *Lady Chatterley's Lover* (1928), whose explicit sexual content resulted in it being censored for many years.

Michèle Le Doeuff (b. 1948) is a French philosopher and feminist writer, best known for *Hipparchia's Choice: An Essay Concerning Women, Philosophy, Etc.* (1991) and *The Sex of Knowing* (1998).

Claude Lévi-Strauss (1908–2009) was a French ethnologist and anthropologist, and is frequently cited as the "father of modern anthropology."

Elaine Marks (1930–2001) was a leading authority on French literature, feminist theory, and women's writing, and is best remembered for her groundbreaking books on Simone de Beauvoir and Colette.

Karl Marx (1818–83) was a German political philosopher and economist whose analysis of class relations under capitalism and articulation of a more egalitarian system provided the basis for communism.

François Mauriac (1885–1970) was a French novelist and a laureate of the 1952 Nobel Prize in Literature, who has, however, been criticized for promoting misogynistic views in his novels.

Toril Moi (b. 1953) is a Norwegian-born American feminist writer and de Beauvoir scholar who has written prolifically on de Beauvoir's role in the feminist movement in France and the United States, including *Sexual/Textual Politics* (1985), *Simone de Beauvoir: The Making of an Intellectual Woman* (1994), and *What Is a Woman? And Other Essays* (1999).

Lewis Henry Morgan (1818–81) was an American anthropologist and social theorist. He is best remembered for his claim that the earliest domestic institution (family) was based on matrilineal lines. Members were identified by their mother's lineage, and descent was traced through the mother's family.

Mariam Motamedi-Fraser is reader of sociology at Goldsmiths (University of London), and is best known for her writings on Islam and the Middle East, feminist theory, and sexuality.

Henry de Motherlant (1895–1972) was a French writer renowned for his misogynistic views, exemplified in his series of four anti-feminist novels, *Les Jeunes Filles* (*The Young Girls*). De Beauvoir devoted an entire chapter of *The Second Sex* to a discussion of his anti-feminist stance.

Andrea Nye (b. 1939) is a feminist writer and philosopher best known for her writings on feminist philosophy, including *Words of Power: A Feminist Reading of the History of Logic* (1990) and *Feminism and Modern Philosophy: An Introduction* (2004).

Judith Okely (b. 1941) is Emeritus Professor of Sociology and Anthropology at the University of Hull. She is best known for her writings on Simone de Beauvoir, as well as her work on identity, autobiography, and anthropological practice.

Camille Paglia (b. 1947) is an American social critic, academic, and "dissident" feminist best known for her harsh criticism of feminist academia and women's studies, her controversial stance on many feminist issues, and her veneration of Simone de Beauvoir.

H. M. Parshley (1884–1953) was the first translator of *The Second Sex*. His English translation has been criticized for cutting out substantial portions of the original, and for often translating terms such as "human" as "man" and "humankind" as "mankind," perpetuating the male-centrism de Beauvoir's book was critiquing.

Pussy Riot: a Russian feminist punk-rock group that protests against the oppression of women, as well the leadership of their government.

Catherine Rodgers is associate professor of languages, translation, and communication at Swansea University in Wales. She writes on contemporary French women's writing, feminist theory, Marguerite Duras, and Simone de Beauvoir.

Jean-Paul Sartre (1905–80) was a leading French existential philosopher, and de Beauvoir's lifetime partner and colleague. His work relied heavily on the idea that individuals are "condemned to be free," and that there is no creator.

William Shakespeare (1564–1616) was an English playwright, actor, and poet, and regarded as one of the most eminent English-language writers to have ever lived. His plays include *Romeo and Juliet*, *Hamlet*, *Macbeth*, *Othello*, and *King Lear* as well as *The Taming of the Shrew*.

Margaret Simons is an American feminist philosopher and critic who has written widely on de Beauvoir and feminist criticism as a whole.

Dorothy E. Smith (b. 1926) is a Canadian sociologist, feminist, and women's studies theorist, and one of the founders of the sociological sub-disciplines of feminist standpoint theory (which traces authority back to individuals' knowledge) and institutional ethnography (which maps individuals' relations within social institutions such as the workplace).

Mary Spongber is an Australian academic specializing in feminist theory, modern history, and women's history, and the editor of the international journal *Australian Feminist Studies*. She is also the author of *Feminizing Venereal Disease* (1995).

Joseph Stalin (1878–1953) was one of the leaders of the Russian Revolution in 1917, and the leader of the Soviet Union from the mid-1920s until his death in 1953.

Stendhal (1783–1842) was the pen name of Marie-Henri Beyle, a nineteenth-century French writer, best remembered for his novels *The Charterhouse of Parma* (1839) and *The Red and the Black* (1830).

Janna Thompson is professor of philosophy at La Trobe University in Australia. She writes on political philosophy, human rights, feminist theory, and ethics.

Natasha Walter (b. 1967) is a feminist writer and activist best known for her books *The New Feminism* (1998) and *Living Dolls: The Return of Sexism* (2010).

Naomi Wolf (b. 1962) is a contemporary feminist critic, journalist, and writer best known for leading what she retrospectively called third-wave feminism, and for her book *The Beauty Myth* (1991).

Mary Wollstonecraft (1759–97) was an English philosopher, writer, and advocate of women's rights, best known for *A Vindication of the Rights of Woman* (1792), in which she championed women's right to an education.

Virginia Woolf (1882–1941) was an English novelist and essayist known for her innovative, experimental writing style and her radical views on women. She is best known for novels such as *Mrs Dalloway* (1925) and *Orlando* (1928), and for her feminist essay *A Room of One's Own* (1929).

WORKS CITED

WORKS CITED

Appignanesi, Lisa. *Simone de Beauvoir*. London: Haus, 2005.

Audet, Jean-Raymond. *Simone de Beauvoir face à la morte.* Lausanne: Éditions L'Age de L'Homme, 1979.

Bair, Deirdre. *Simone de Beauvoir: A Biography.* London: Cape, 1991.

Bates, Laura. *Everyday Sexism*. London: Simon & Schuster, 2014.

Bauer, Nancy. "Must We Read de Beauvoir?" In *The Legacy of Simone de Beauvoir*, edited by Emily Grosholz. New York: Oxford University Press, 2004.

Beauvoir, Simone de. *Pyrrhus et Cinnin*. Paris: Gallimard, 1944.

The Second Sex. Translated by H. M. Parshley. New York: Vintage, 1953.

She Came to Stay. Translated by Roger Senhouse and Yvonne Moyse. New York: W. W. Norton & Co.,1954 (English translation of *L'Invitée*. Paris: Gallimard, 1943).

Lettres à Sartre (*Letters to Sartre*). Edited by Sylvie le Bon. Paris: Gallimard, 1990.

The Mandarins. Translated by Leonard M. Friedman. New York: W. W. Norton & Co., 1991 (English translation of *Les mandarins*. Paris: Gallimard, 1954).

The Ethics of Ambiguity. Translated by Bernard Frechtman. New York: Citadel Press, 1996 (English translation of *Pour une morale de l'ambiguité*. Paris: Gallimard, 1947).

Bebel, August. *Women and Socialism*. Translated by Meta L. Stern. New York: Socialist Literature Company and Co-operative Press, 1910.

Bergoffen, Debra. "(Re)counting the Sexual Difference." In *The Cambridge Companion to Simone de Beauvoir,* edited by Claudia Card, 248–65. Cambridge: Cambridge University Press, 2003.

Berkowitz, Eric. *Sex and Punishment: Four Thousand Years of Judging Desire*. Berkeley, CA: Counterpoint, 2012.

Butler, Judith. "Sex and Gender in Simone de Beauvoir's Second Sex." *Yale French Studies* 72 (1986): 35–49.

Gender Trouble: Feminism and the Subversion of Identity. London: Routledge, 1990.

Chaperon, Sylvie. *Les années Beauvoir: 1945–1970* (*The Beauvoir Years: 1945–1970*. Paris: Fayard, 2000.

Daigle, Christine, and Jacob Golomb, eds. *Sartre and Beauvoir: The Question of Influence*. Bloomington, IN: Indiana University Press, 2009.

Evans, Alfred B. *Soviet Marxism-Leninism: The Decline of an Ideology*. Westport, CT: Praeger, 1993.

Evans, Ruth, ed. *Simone de Beauvoir's* The Second Sex*: New Interdisciplinary Essays*. Manchester: Manchester University Press, 1998.

Fallaize, Elizabeth, ed. *Simone de Beauvoir: A Critical Reader*. New York: Routledge, 1998.

Fullbrook, Edward, and Kate Fullbrook. *Sex and Philosophy: Re-thinking de Beauvoir and Sartre*. London: Bloomsbury, 2008.

Gatens, Moira. "De Beauvoir and Biology: A Second Look." In *The Cambridge Companion to Simone de Beauvoir,* edited by Claudia Card, 266–85. Cambridge: Cambridge University Press, 2003.

Gerassi, John. "Interview with Simone de Beauvoir: *The Second Sex*, 25 Years Later." *Society*, January–February (1976). Accessed May 5, 2015. www.marxists.org/reference/subject/ethics/de-beauvoir/1976/interview.htm.

Grosholz, Emily. *The Legacy of Simone de Beauvoir*. Oxford: Oxford University Press, 2006.

Hains, Rebecca. *The Princess Problem: Guiding Our Girls through the Princess-obsessed Years*. Naperville, IL: Sourcebooks, 2014.

Holveck, Eleanore. *Simone de Beauvoir's Philosophy of Lived Experience*. New York: Rowman & Littlefield, 2002.

Hutchison, Karina, and Fiona Jenkins. *Women in Philosophy: What Needs to Change?* Oxford: Oxford University Press, 2013.

Jones, James H. *Alfred C. Kinsey: A Public/Private Life.* New York: Norton, 1997.

Kelly-Gadol, Joan. "The Social Relation of the Sexes: Methodological Implications of Women's History." In *Feminism and Methodology: Social Science Issues,* edited by Sandra G. Harding. Bloomington and Indianapolis, IN: Indiana University Press, 1987,

Kinsey, Alfred C., Wardell B. Pomeroy, and Paul H. Gebhard. *Sexual Behavior in the Human* Male. Bloomington, IN: Indiana University Press, 1975.

Sexual Behavior in the Human Female. Bloomington, IN: Indiana University Press, 1998.

Kruks, Sonia. *Simone de Beauvoir and the Politics of Ambiguity*. Oxford: Oxford University Press, 2012.

Ladenson, Elizabeth. "Censorship." In *The Book: A Global History*, edited by

Michael F. Suarez and H. R. Wooudhuysen, 164–82. Oxford: Oxford University Press, 2013.

Laubier, Claire. *The Condition of Women in France: 1945 to the Present – A Documentary Anthology*. London: Routledge, 1992.

Le Doeuff, Michèle *Hipparchia's Choice*. Translated by Trista Selous. New York: Columbia University Press, 1990.

Leighton, Jean. *Simone de Beauvoir and Women.* Madison, NJ: Farleigh Dickinson University Press, 1975.

Moi, Toril. *Simone de Beauvoir: The Making of an Intellectual Woman*. New York: Oxford University Press, 1994.

What Is a Woman? Oxford and New York: Oxford University Press, 1999.

Sexual/Textual Politics. London and New York: Routledge, 2002.

"The Adulteress Wife." *London Review of Books* 32, no. 3. (February 11, 2010). Accessed February 2, 2015. www.lrb.co.uk/v32/n03/toril-moi/the-adulteress-wife.

Monogan, Sharmon Lynette. "Patriarchy: Perpetuating the Practice of Female Genital Mutilation." *International Research Journal of Arts & Humanities* 37 (2010): 83–99.

Motamedi-Fraser, Mariam. *Identity Without Selfhood: Simone de Beauvoir and Sexuality.* Cambridge: Cambridge Cultural Social Studies, 1999.

Muel-Dreyfus, Francine. *Vichy et L'Éternel Feminin.* Paris: Editions du Seuil, 1996.

Nye, Andrea. *Feminist Theory and the Philosophies of Man*. London: Routledge, 2013.

Orenstein, Peggy. *Cinderella Ate My Daughter: Dispatches from the Front Lines of the New Girlie-Girl Culture*. New York: Harper, 2011.

Paglia, Camille. *Sex, Art and American Culture: Essays*. New York: Penguin Books, 1992.

Pilardy, Jo-Ann. "Feminists Read *The Second* Sex." In *Feminist Interpretations of Simone de Beauvoir,* edited by Margaret A. Simons. University Park, PA: Pennsylvania State University Press, 1995.

Poweroy, Wardell. *Dr Kinsey and the Institute for Sex Research*. New Haven, CT: Yale University Press, 1982.

Rodgers, Catherine. "The Influence of *The Second Sex* on the French Feminist Scene." In *Simone de Beauvoir's* The Second Sex*: New Interdisciplinary Essays*, edited by Ruth Evans. Manchester: Manchester University Press, 1998.

Rowbotham, Sheila. "Foreword." In Simone de Beauvoir, *The Second Sex*, translated by Candace Borde and Sheila Malovany-Chevalier. New York: Vintage, 2009.

Sartre, Jean-Paul. *Anti-semite and Jew: An Exploration of the Etiology of Hate*. Translated by George Becker. New York: Schocken, 1948 (English translation of *Réflexions sur la question juive*. Paris: Éditions Morihien, 1944).

"Orphée Noire." In *Anthologie de la Nouvelle poésie nègre et malgache de langue francaise*, edited by Leopold S. Senghor. Paris: Presse Universitaires de France, 1977.

"Existentialism and Humanism." In *Jean-Paul Sartre: Basic Writings*, edited by Stephen Priest, 20–57. New York: Routledge, 2002.

Scarth, Fredrika. *The Other Within: Ethics, Politics and the Body in Simone de Beauvoir*. New York: Rowman & Littlefield, 2004.

Schwarzer, Alice. "The Revolutionary Woman." In *After the Second Sex: Conversations with Simone de* Beauvoir. London: Pantheon, 1984.

Servan-Schreiber, Jean-Louis. "Why I Am a Feminist: Interview with Simone de Beauvoir [1975]." Accessed March 5, 2015. www.youtube.com/watch?v=v2LkME3MMNk.

Simons, Margaret A. "The Silencing of Simone de Beauvoir: Guess What's Missing from *The Second Sex*." *Women's Studies International Forum* 6, no. 6 (1983): 559–664.

"*The Second Sex*: From Marxism to Radical Feminism." In *Feminist Interpretations of Simone de Beauvoir,* edited by Margaret A. Simons, 243–62. University Park, PA: Pennsylvania State University Press, 1995.

"Is *The Second Sex* Beauvoir's Application of Sartrean Existentialism?" Paper given at the Twentieth World Congress of Philosophy, Boston, MA, August 10–15, 1998.

Beauvoir and the Second Sex: Feminism, Race and the Origins of Existentialism. Oxford: Rowman & Littlefield, 1999.

ed. *Feminist Interpretations of Simone de Beauvoir*. University Park, PA: Pennsylvania State University Press, 1995.

Simons, Margaret A., and Jessica Benjamin. "Beauvoir Interview (1979)." In *Beauvoir and the Second Sex*, edited by Margaret A. Simons, 1–22. New York: Rowman & Littlefield, 2001.

Smith, Dorothy E. *The Everyday World as Problematic: A Feminist Sociology*. Boston: Northeastern University Press, 1987.

Spelman, Elisabeth. *Inessential Woman: Problems of Exclusion in Feminist Thought.* Boston: Beacon Press, 1988.

Spongber, Mary. *Writing Women's History since the Renaissance.* New York: Palgrave Macmillan, 2002.

Thompson, Janna. *Women and Philosophy.* Bundoora: Australasian Association of Philosophy, 1986.

Tidd, Ursula. *Simone de Beauvoir*. London: Routledge, 2004.

Underwood, Gill, and Khursheed Wadia. *Women and Politics in France: 1958–2000.* London and New York: Routledge, 2000.

Walters, Natasha. *Living Dolls: The Return of Sexism*. London: Virago, 2010.

Woolf, Virginia. *A Room of One's Own*. London and New York: Penguin, 2002.

THE MACAT LIBRARY
BY DISCIPLINE

AFRICANA STUDIES

Chinua Achebe's *An Image of Africa: Racism in Conrad's Heart of Darkness*
W. E. B. Du Bois's *The Souls of Black Folk*
Zora Neale Huston's *Characteristics of Negro Expression*
Martin Luther King Jr's *Why We Can't Wait*
Toni Morrison's *Playing in the Dark: Whiteness in the American Literary Imagination*

ANTHROPOLOGY

Arjun Appadurai's *Modernity at Large: Cultural Dimensions of Globalisation*
Philippe Ariès's *Centuries of Childhood*
Franz Boas's *Race, Language and Culture*
Kim Chan & Renée Mauborgne's *Blue Ocean Strategy*
Jared Diamond's *Guns, Germs & Steel: the Fate of Human Societies*
Jared Diamond's *Collapse: How Societies Choose to Fail or Survive*
E. E. Evans-Pritchard's *Witchcraft, Oracles and Magic Among the Azande*
James Ferguson's *The Anti-Politics Machine*
Clifford Geertz's *The Interpretation of Cultures*
David Graeber's *Debt: the First 5000 Years*
Karen Ho's *Liquidated: An Ethnography of Wall Street*
Geert Hofstede's *Culture's Consequences: Comparing Values, Behaviors, Institutes and Organizations across Nations*
Claude Lévi-Strauss's *Structural Anthropology*
Jay Macleod's *Ain't No Makin' It: Aspirations and Attainment in a Low-Income Neighborhood*
Saba Mahmood's *The Politics of Piety: The Islamic Revival and the Feminist Subject*
Marcel Mauss's *The Gift*

BUSINESS

Jean Lave & Etienne Wenger's *Situated Learning*
Theodore Levitt's *Marketing Myopia*
Burton G. Malkiel's *A Random Walk Down Wall Street*
Douglas McGregor's *The Human Side of Enterprise*
Michael Porter's *Competitive Strategy: Creating and Sustaining Superior Performance*
John Kotter's *Leading Change*
C. K. Prahalad & Gary Hamel's *The Core Competence of the Corporation*

CRIMINOLOGY

Michelle Alexander's *The New Jim Crow: Mass Incarceration in the Age of Colorblindness*
Michael R. Gottfredson & Travis Hirschi's *A General Theory of Crime*
Richard Herrnstein & Charles A. Murray's *The Bell Curve: Intelligence and Class Structure in American Life*
Elizabeth Loftus's *Eyewitness Testimony*
Jay Macleod's *Ain't No Makin' It: Aspirations and Attainment in a Low-Income Neighborhood*
Philip Zimbardo's *The Lucifer Effect*

ECONOMICS

Janet Abu-Lughod's *Before European Hegemony*
Ha-Joon Chang's *Kicking Away the Ladder*
David Brion Davis's *The Problem of Slavery in the Age of Revolution*
Milton Friedman's *The Role of Monetary Policy*
Milton Friedman's *Capitalism and Freedom*
David Graeber's *Debt: the First 5000 Years*
Friedrich Hayek's *The Road to Serfdom*
Karen Ho's *Liquidated: An Ethnography of Wall Street*

John Maynard Keynes's *The General Theory of Employment, Interest and Money*
Charles P. Kindleberger's *Manias, Panics and Crashes*
Robert Lucas's *Why Doesn't Capital Flow from Rich to Poor Countries?*
Burton G. Malkiel's *A Random Walk Down Wall Street*
Thomas Robert Malthus's *An Essay on the Principle of Population*
Karl Marx's *Capital*
Thomas Piketty's *Capital in the Twenty-First Century*
Amartya Sen's *Development as Freedom*
Adam Smith's *The Wealth of Nations*
Nassim Nicholas Taleb's *The Black Swan: The Impact of the Highly Improbable*
Amos Tversky's & Daniel Kahneman's *Judgment under Uncertainty: Heuristics and Biases*
Mahbub Ul Haq's *Reflections on Human Development*
Max Weber's *The Protestant Ethic and the Spirit of Capitalism*

FEMINISM AND GENDER STUDIES

Judith Butler's *Gender Trouble*
Simone De Beauvoir's *The Second Sex*
Michel Foucault's *History of Sexuality*
Betty Friedan's *The Feminine Mystique*
Saba Mahmood's *The Politics of Piety: The Islamic Revival and the Feminist Subject*
Joan Wallach Scott's *Gender and the Politics of History*
Mary Wollstonecraft's *A Vindication of the Rights of Woman*
Virginia Woolf's *A Room of One's Own*

GEOGRAPHY

The Brundtland Report's *Our Common Future*
Rachel Carson's *Silent Spring*
Charles Darwin's *On the Origin of Species*
James Ferguson's *The Anti-Politics Machine*
Jane Jacobs's *The Death and Life of Great American Cities*
James Lovelock's *Gaia: A New Look at Life on Earth*
Amartya Sen's *Development as Freedom*
Mathis Wackernagel & William Rees's *Our Ecological Footprint*

HISTORY

Janet Abu-Lughod's *Before European Hegemony*
Benedict Anderson's *Imagined Communities*
Bernard Bailyn's *The Ideological Origins of the American Revolution*
Hanna Batatu's *The Old Social Classes And The Revolutionary Movements Of Iraq*
Christopher Browning's *Ordinary Men: Reserve Police Batallion 101 and the Final Solution in Poland*
Edmund Burke's *Reflections on the Revolution in France*
William Cronon's *Nature's Metropolis: Chicago And The Great West*
Alfred W. Crosby's *The Columbian Exchange*
Hamid Dabashi's *Iran: A People Interrupted*
David Brion Davis's *The Problem of Slavery in the Age of Revolution*
Nathalie Zemon Davis's *The Return of Martin Guerre*
Jared Diamond's *Guns, Germs & Steel: the Fate of Human Societies*
Frank Dikotter's *Mao's Great Famine*
John W Dower's *War Without Mercy: Race And Power In The Pacific War*
W. E. B. Du Bois's *The Souls of Black Folk*
Richard J. Evans's *In Defence of History*
Lucien Febvre's *The Problem of Unbelief in the 16th Century*
Sheila Fitzpatrick's *Everyday Stalinism*

The Macat Library By Discipline

Eric Foner's *Reconstruction: America's Unfinished Revolution, 1863-1877*
Michel Foucault's *Discipline and Punish*
Michel Foucault's *History of Sexuality*
Francis Fukuyama's *The End of History and the Last Man*
John Lewis Gaddis's *We Now Know: Rethinking Cold War History*
Ernest Gellner's *Nations and Nationalism*
Eugene Genovese's *Roll, Jordan, Roll: The World the Slaves Made*
Carlo Ginzburg's *The Night Battles*
Daniel Goldhagen's *Hitler's Willing Executioners*
Jack Goldstone's *Revolution and Rebellion in the Early Modern World*
Antonio Gramsci's *The Prison Notebooks*
Alexander Hamilton, John Jay & James Madison's *The Federalist Papers*
Christopher Hill's *The World Turned Upside Down*
Carole Hillenbrand's *The Crusades: Islamic Perspectives*
Thomas Hobbes's *Leviathan*
Eric Hobsbawm's *The Age Of Revolution*
John A. Hobson's *Imperialism: A Study*
Albert Hourani's *History of the Arab Peoples*
Samuel P. Huntington's *The Clash of Civilizations and the Remaking of World Order*
C. L. R. James's *The Black Jacobins*
Tony Judt's *Postwar: A History of Europe Since 1945*
Ernst Kantorowicz's *The King's Two Bodies: A Study in Medieval Political Theology*
Paul Kennedy's *The Rise and Fall of the Great Powers*
Ian Kershaw's *The "Hitler Myth": Image and Reality in the Third Reich*
John Maynard Keynes's *The General Theory of Employment, Interest and Money*
Charles P. Kindleberger's *Manias, Panics and Crashes*
Martin Luther King Jr's *Why We Can't Wait*
Henry Kissinger's *World Order: Reflections on the Character of Nations and the Course of History*
Thomas Kuhn's *The Structure of Scientific Revolutions*
Georges Lefebvre's *The Coming of the French Revolution*
John Locke's *Two Treatises of Government*
Niccolò Machiavelli's *The Prince*
Thomas Robert Malthus's *An Essay on the Principle of Population*
Mahmood Mamdani's *Citizen and Subject: Contemporary Africa And The Legacy Of Late Colonialism*
Karl Marx's *Capital*
Stanley Milgram's *Obedience to Authority*
John Stuart Mill's *On Liberty*
Thomas Paine's *Common Sense*
Thomas Paine's *Rights of Man*
Geoffrey Parker's *Global Crisis: War, Climate Change and Catastrophe in the Seventeenth Century*
Jonathan Riley-Smith's *The First Crusade and the Idea of Crusading*
Jean-Jacques Rousseau's *The Social Contract*
Joan Wallach Scott's *Gender and the Politics of History*
Theda Skocpol's *States and Social Revolutions*
Adam Smith's *The Wealth of Nations*
Timothy Snyder's *Bloodlands: Europe Between Hitler and Stalin*
Sun Tzu's *The Art of War*
Keith Thomas's *Religion and the Decline of Magic*
Thucydides's *The History of the Peloponnesian War*
Frederick Jackson Turner's *The Significance of the Frontier in American History*
Odd Arne Westad's *The Global Cold War: Third World Interventions And The Making Of Our Times*

LITERATURE

Chinua Achebe's *An Image of Africa: Racism in Conrad's Heart of Darkness*
Roland Barthes's *Mythologies*
Homi K. Bhabha's *The Location of Culture*
Judith Butler's *Gender Trouble*
Simone De Beauvoir's *The Second Sex*
Ferdinand De Saussure's *Course in General Linguistics*
T. S. Eliot's *The Sacred Wood: Essays on Poetry and Criticism*
Zora Neale Huston's *Characteristics of Negro Expression*
Toni Morrison's *Playing in the Dark: Whiteness in the American Literary Imagination*
Edward Said's *Orientalism*
Gayatri Chakravorty Spivak's *Can the Subaltern Speak?*
Mary Wollstonecraft's *A Vindication of the Rights of Women*
Virginia Woolf's *A Room of One's Own*

PHILOSOPHY

Elizabeth Anscombe's *Modern Moral Philosophy*
Hannah Arendt's *The Human Condition*
Aristotle's *Metaphysics*
Aristotle's *Nicomachean Ethics*
Edmund Gettier's *Is Justified True Belief Knowledge?*
Georg Wilhelm Friedrich Hegel's *Phenomenology of Spirit*
David Hume's *Dialogues Concerning Natural Religion*
David Hume's *The Enquiry for Human Understanding*
Immanuel Kant's *Religion within the Boundaries of Mere Reason*
Immanuel Kant's *Critique of Pure Reason*
Søren Kierkegaard's *The Sickness Unto Death*
Søren Kierkegaard's *Fear and Trembling*
C. S. Lewis's *The Abolition of Man*
Alasdair MacIntyre's *After Virtue*
Marcus Aurelius's *Meditations*
Friedrich Nietzsche's *On the Genealogy of Morality*
Friedrich Nietzsche's *Beyond Good and Evil*
Plato's *Republic*
Plato's *Symposium*
Jean-Jacques Rousseau's *The Social Contract*
Gilbert Ryle's *The Concept of Mind*
Baruch Spinoza's *Ethics*
Sun Tzu's *The Art of War*
Ludwig Wittgenstein's *Philosophical Investigations*

POLITICS

Benedict Anderson's *Imagined Communities*
Aristotle's *Politics*
Bernard Bailyn's *The Ideological Origins of the American Revolution*
Edmund Burke's *Reflections on the Revolution in France*
John C. Calhoun's *A Disquisition on Government*
Ha-Joon Chang's *Kicking Away the Ladder*
Hamid Dabashi's *Iran: A People Interrupted*
Hamid Dabashi's *Theology of Discontent: The Ideological Foundation of the Islamic Revolution in Iran*
Robert Dahl's *Democracy and its Critics*
Robert Dahl's *Who Governs?*
David Brion Davis's *The Problem of Slavery in the Age of Revolution*

The Macat Library By Discipline

Alexis De Tocqueville's *Democracy in America*
James Ferguson's *The Anti-Politics Machine*
Frank Dikotter's *Mao's Great Famine*
Sheila Fitzpatrick's *Everyday Stalinism*
Eric Foner's *Reconstruction: America's Unfinished Revolution, 1863-1877*
Milton Friedman's *Capitalism and Freedom*
Francis Fukuyama's *The End of History and the Last Man*
John Lewis Gaddis's *We Now Know: Rethinking Cold War History*
Ernest Gellner's *Nations and Nationalism*
David Graeber's *Debt: the First 5000 Years*
Antonio Gramsci's *The Prison Notebooks*
Alexander Hamilton, John Jay & James Madison's *The Federalist Papers*
Friedrich Hayek's *The Road to Serfdom*
Christopher Hill's *The World Turned Upside Down*
Thomas Hobbes's *Leviathan*
John A. Hobson's *Imperialism: A Study*
Samuel P. Huntington's *The Clash of Civilizations and the Remaking of World Order*
Tony Judt's *Postwar: A History of Europe Since 1945*
David C. Kang's *China Rising: Peace, Power and Order in East Asia*
Paul Kennedy's *The Rise and Fall of Great Powers*
Robert Keohane's *After Hegemony*
Martin Luther King Jr.'s *Why We Can't Wait*
Henry Kissinger's *World Order: Reflections on the Character of Nations and the Course of History*
John Locke's *Two Treatises of Government*
Niccolò Machiavelli's *The Prince*
Thomas Robert Malthus's *An Essay on the Principle of Population*
Mahmood Mamdani's *Citizen and Subject: Contemporary Africa And The Legacy Of Late Colonialism*
Karl Marx's *Capital*
John Stuart Mill's *On Liberty*
John Stuart Mill's *Utilitarianism*
Hans Morgenthau's *Politics Among Nations*
Thomas Paine's *Common Sense*
Thomas Paine's *Rights of Man*
Thomas Piketty's *Capital in the Twenty-First Century*
Robert D. Putman's *Bowling Alone*
John Rawls's *Theory of Justice*
Jean-Jacques Rousseau's *The Social Contract*
Theda Skocpol's *States and Social Revolutions*
Adam Smith's *The Wealth of Nations*
Sun Tzu's *The Art of War*
Henry David Thoreau's *Civil Disobedience*
Thucydides's *The History of the Peloponnesian War*
Kenneth Waltz's *Theory of International Politics*
Max Weber's *Politics as a Vocation*
Odd Arne Westad's *The Global Cold War: Third World Interventions And The Making Of Our Times*

POSTCOLONIAL STUDIES

Roland Barthes's *Mythologies*
Frantz Fanon's *Black Skin, White Masks*
Homi K. Bhabha's *The Location of Culture*
Gustavo Gutiérrez's *A Theology of Liberation*
Edward Said's *Orientalism*
Gayatri Chakravorty Spivak's *Can the Subaltern Speak?*

PSYCHOLOGY

Gordon Allport's *The Nature of Prejudice*
Alan Baddeley & Graham Hitch's *Aggression: A Social Learning Analysis*
Albert Bandura's *Aggression: A Social Learning Analysis*
Leon Festinger's *A Theory of Cognitive Dissonance*
Sigmund Freud's *The Interpretation of Dreams*
Betty Friedan's *The Feminine Mystique*
Michael R. Gottfredson & Travis Hirschi's *A General Theory of Crime*
Eric Hoffer's *The True Believer: Thoughts on the Nature of Mass Movements*
William James's *Principles of Psychology*
Elizabeth Loftus's *Eyewitness Testimony*
A. H. Maslow's *A Theory of Human Motivation*
Stanley Milgram's *Obedience to Authority*
Steven Pinker's *The Better Angels of Our Nature*
Oliver Sacks's *The Man Who Mistook His Wife For a Hat*
Richard Thaler & Cass Sunstein's *Nudge: Improving Decisions About Health, Wealth and Happiness*
Amos Tversky's *Judgment under Uncertainty: Heuristics and Biases*
Philip Zimbardo's *The Lucifer Effect*

SCIENCE

Rachel Carson's *Silent Spring*
William Cronon's *Nature's Metropolis: Chicago And The Great West*
Alfred W. Crosby's *The Columbian Exchange*
Charles Darwin's *On the Origin of Species*
Richard Dawkin's *The Selfish Gene*
Thomas Kuhn's *The Structure of Scientific Revolutions*
Geoffrey Parker's *Global Crisis: War, Climate Change and Catastrophe in the Seventeenth Century*
Mathis Wackernagel & William Rees's *Our Ecological Footprint*

SOCIOLOGY

Michelle Alexander's *The New Jim Crow: Mass Incarceration in the Age of Colorblindness*
Gordon Allport's *The Nature of Prejudice*
Albert Bandura's *Aggression: A Social Learning Analysis*
Hanna Batatu's *The Old Social Classes And The Revolutionary Movements Of Iraq*
Ha-Joon Chang's *Kicking Away the Ladder*
W. E. B. Du Bois's *The Souls of Black Folk*
Émile Durkheim's *On Suicide*
Frantz Fanon's *Black Skin, White Masks*
Frantz Fanon's *The Wretched of the Earth*
Eric Foner's *Reconstruction: America's Unfinished Revolution, 1863-1877*
Eugene Genovese's *Roll, Jordan, Roll: The World the Slaves Made*
Jack Goldstone's *Revolution and Rebellion in the Early Modern World*
Antonio Gramsci's *The Prison Notebooks*
Richard Herrnstein & Charles A Murray's *The Bell Curve: Intelligence and Class Structure in American Life*
Eric Hoffer's *The True Believer: Thoughts on the Nature of Mass Movements*
Jane Jacobs's *The Death and Life of Great American Cities*
Robert Lucas's *Why Doesn't Capital Flow from Rich to Poor Countries?*
Jay Macleod's *Ain't No Makin' It: Aspirations and Attainment in a Low Income Neighborhood*
Elaine May's *Homeward Bound: American Families in the Cold War Era*
Douglas McGregor's *The Human Side of Enterprise*
C. Wright Mills's *The Sociological Imagination*

The Macat Library By Discipline

Thomas Piketty's *Capital in the Twenty-First Century*
Robert D. Putman's *Bowling Alone*
David Riesman's *The Lonely Crowd: A Study of the Changing American Character*
Edward Said's *Orientalism*
Joan Wallach Scott's *Gender and the Politics of History*
Theda Skocpol's *States and Social Revolutions*
Max Weber's *The Protestant Ethic and the Spirit of Capitalism*

THEOLOGY

Augustine's *Confessions*
Benedict's *Rule of St Benedict*
Gustavo Gutiérrez's *A Theology of Liberation*
Carole Hillenbrand's *The Crusades: Islamic Perspectives*
David Hume's *Dialogues Concerning Natural Religion*
Immanuel Kant's *Religion within the Boundaries of Mere Reason*
Ernst Kantorowicz's *The King's Two Bodies: A Study in Medieval Political Theology*
Søren Kierkegaard's *The Sickness Unto Death*
C. S. Lewis's *The Abolition of Man*
Saba Mahmood's *The Politics of Piety: The Islamic Revival and the Feminist Subjec*t
Baruch Spinoza's *Ethics*
Keith Thomas's *Religion and the Decline of Magic*

COMING SOON

Chris Argyris's *The Individual and the Organisation*
Seyla Benhabib's *The Rights of Others*
Walter Benjamin's *The Work Of Art in the Age of Mechanical Reproduction*
John Berger's *Ways of Seeing*
Pierre Bourdieu's *Outline of a Theory of Practice*
Mary Douglas's *Purity and Danger*
Roland Dworkin's *Taking Rights Seriously*
James G. March's *Exploration and Exploitation in Organisational Learning*
Ikujiro Nonaka's *A Dynamic Theory of Organizational Knowledge Creation*
Griselda Pollock's *Vision and Difference*
Amartya Sen's *Inequality Re-Examined*
Susan Sontag's *On Photography*
Yasser Tabbaa's *The Transformation of Islamic Art*
Ludwig von Mises's *Theory of Money and Credit*

Printed in the United States
by Baker & Taylor Publisher Services